tales from the toolbox

Inside a Professional Cycling Team

BY SCOTT PARR with Rupert Guinness

VELOPRESS • BOULDER, COLORADO

In memory of Fabio

Tales from the Toolbox
Copyright © 1997 Scott Parr

Library of Congress Cataloging-in-Publication Data

Parr, Scott, 1969-
    Tales from the toolbox : inside a pro cycling team / by Scott Parr
with Rupert Guinness.
      p.   cm.
    ISBN 1-884737-39-0 (pbk.)
    1. Motorola Cycling Team--History. 2. Bicycle racing--Europe-History.
    I. Guinness, Rupert. II. Title.
GV1047.M68P37   1997
796.6'2'092--dc21
[B]   97-26360
                                          CIP

PRINTED IN THE USA

Cover photo by Beth Schneider
Design by Erin Johnson

VELO *press*

1830 N. 55th Street • Boulder, Colorado • 80301-2700 • USA
303/440-0601 • FAX 303/444-6788 • E-MAIL velo@7dogs.com

To purchase additional copies of this book or other Velo products,
call 800/234-8356 or visit us on the Web at www.velocatalogue.com

CONTENTS

Foreword

by Steve Bauer, Professional Cyclist 1984-1996

The rain had been plummeting down, blown by blustery winds, the entire day. The wet, slick and narrow descent at Chambéry, France, had made the 1989 World Professional Road Race Championship as mentally exhausting as it was physically demanding.

About 10 riders remained in the decimated peloton, which included Greg LeMond, Sean Kelly, Laurent Fignon, Claude Criquielion and me. A small leading group began the final climb some 30 seconds or so in front of us. Our group followed with unrelenting intent and focus, the adrenaline attempting to overcome the imminent fatigue from the previous seven hours of grueling and repetitive ascents and descents of the championship course.

Side by side, we all shifted our weight back and forth rhythmically as we climbed the steepest gradient of the mountain, each of us waiting for one to make the move to bridge across to the leaders. Then there was an attack from Fignon…. We all hesitated, and the intensity mounted one more notch as the rest of us continued the climb with our tactical plans poised for our final moves.

Fignon was going well and made it into the front group; and suddenly, LeMond, who had not looked good all day, blasted away one kilometer from the top of the climb. Then Kelly went — that was it! I responded with all the force my body and legs could muster. I was gathering momentum, but was too slow. I had to make it happen ... now! Surging, I started to pass struggling riders, and in a few seconds I blasted past Kelly, his muscles full with lactic acid and trying to hold his speed. At my absolute best, I was now charging in on LeMond's heels, as his back just disappeared over the crest of the climb. Within seconds, I crossed the top of the climb for the last time ... and my visions zeroed in on the leaders as LeMond joined them.

"I'm here," I thought, as I sucked in huge volumes of air to recuperate from the maximum effort and prepare for the calculating race to the finish. Then ... Ppppssssssss! My tire had punctured and I was struck with total disbelief! It was a shocking realization that, in an instant, the greatest race I had ever ridden was over. At the peak of my career, fitness and capabilities, fate had defeated me.

The support motorcycle carrying a wheel-change mechanic jumped into action on the spot. The rear wheel change was efficient and I was on my way. In any other lap, such an excellent wheel change from the mechanic would have kept my world championship hopes alive. Yet, with five kilometers to go in this race, not even the most experienced hands of a Scott Parr could have saved me.

Professional mechanics are the glue of a cycling team. It is rare that they are in the limelight with a heroic, on-the-money wheel change, of which they could claim some fame for the subsequent victory. However, these dedicated souls are the boys of the team from whom we get our wheels — from rolling out of the box and into first gear, to the moment we need absolute overdrive.

Day in, day out, every cycling season, we rely on these guys who hand us our bikes each new race day, ready to perform without failure. Without failure? Yes, I can honestly say that in 12 years of professional bicycle racing my bike never failed me. Of course, I had my share of flat tires and some rare breakages; but a bike failure never cost me a win.

The team mechanics work behind the scenes. They are the last to the dinner table and the earliest to rise in the morning (along with the soigneurs). I lost some incredible races with bad luck, but I never lost a race because my mechanic overlooked something in the preparation of my bike. Considering that I raced an average of 100 to 120 days a year through my 12 years as a pro, I would have to believe that the mechanics working on my bikes must have been pretty damn good.

These guys are under tremendous pressure to perform, just like the athletes. They are under constant stress to ensure that every mechanical detail is perfect, every day, every race; whether it's a stage of the Tour de France or just a small town criterium. The mechanic cannot give his rider a bike with a clear conscience unless he knows that his work is mechanically flawless.

How often do we riders go to the line with the confidence that we have prepared ourselves physically and mentally to perform at the same level as our bicycles will? I guess bicycle racers are not machines, nor is anyone else on the team. However, everyone involved with a professional team has to have a solid character. Behind some tiny European hotel late at night, as a spotlight beams down from the team truck, mechanics have no place, time or energy to claim exception.

For me, their work ethic, dedication and spirit for the sport and the riders they work for is paramount. When they handed me my bicycle in the morning, I knew that I could race that bicycle with the utmost confidence that it would not fail me.

I'm sure that in reading this book you will understand more of the special life of the professional cycling mechanic. It's a life surely not understood very well, but a story Scott Parr has been inspired to tell — from bicycle technicalities to the life of travel and toughness in a professional cycling team. I hope you enjoy it.

Finally, to all the great mechanics who always gave me their absolute best effort: thanks!

— *Steve Bauer*

Introduction and Acknowledgments

It has been almost two years since I first had the idea of writing a book. I can't remember exactly what triggered the original idea, but it came one day in 1995 while driving the team truck down to Spain from Belgium. I knew that my career as a pro mechanic was ending and that this was probably my last year with Motorola and of living in Europe. I was very excited about the idea of getting on with life, and the new adventures that it had in store for me, even though I sensed it probably wouldn't have anything to do with cycling. At the time, there seemed nothing left in the bicycle industry that interested me, or that I felt I wanted to do.

However, it bothered me that, in a way, everything I had learned and experienced in almost seven years as a professional mechanic would be lost. Finally, it came to me that the one way I could pass along some of that knowledge was to write a book. Albeit, when the time came to actually sit down and write, I was at a loss. I was not a writer and always felt that writing had been one of my weakest areas in school. Looking back to the way I felt after committing myself to this book — and actually sitting down for the first time to start chapter one — all I saw in front of me was a blank piece of paper. Where was I to begin? The idea of how much work lay ahead seemed insurmountable. In hindsight, I don't think I ever

truly believed I would finish it. Many times, I contemplated quitting —
and even tried to — but I was convinced to stick with it. The main reason
for continuing was because I knew that if I quit, I would regret taking
the easy way out for the rest of my life. I didn't want to be a quitter.

I can't say that the book has turned out exactly as I had imagined, but then
again I don't know if I really had an idea what the final product would be
like anyway. All I hope is that you will enjoy reading it and learning something about life behind the scenes of a professional cycling team.

You can never achieve what you are aiming for unless you have the
right people behind you, to help and inspire you. I will never forget who
they were in my career as a professional team mechanic. I'd like to thank
Len Pettyjohn, who taught me so much, believed in me enough to give me
my first shot in the professional ranks, and who helped me believe in
myself. There was George Noyes, who gave me the opportunity of a lifetime by helping me get on the Motorola team and adapt to life in Europe,
and put up with me all those years. And then there's Jim Ochowicz, who
built and managed one of the greatest cycling teams in the world, and
took me on board for a most privileged experience. Finally, I would like to
thank Rupert Guinness for his invaluable help in writing this book, and the
editors at VeloPress for preparing it for publication.

— *Scott Parr*
June 1997

chapter one

A Day in the Life

of a Professional Cycling Team Mechanic

'Beep … beep … beep…." It's 6 a.m., and the alarm is jerking me awake. Am I still dreaming? Or is it really time for me to get up? It's no dream. Lying in bed, I try to figure out where the bathroom is in this hotel room. I've walked into many walls on my way to what I thought was the bathroom … and spent just as many mornings calculating how long I can stay in bed without being late for breakfast.

As usual, the calculation isn't a simple one. Then, I start thinking, "What am I doing here?"

It's now been two-and-a-half weeks since the Tour de France began and I'm ready to go home. The fact that four days after the Tour finishes, I leave for another three-week road trip is not even considered. There's no point thinking about that, when the Tour requires you to tackle one day at a time.

After a quick shower, I stumble around the room, hurriedly throwing clothes into my team-issue suitcase. Then, while struggling down the darkened stairway with my packed case in one hand, briefcase in the other, and laundry bag under an arm, I wonder if I will be the last mechanic at breakfast.

After leaving my suitcase at reception, I look for the answer. And with the breakfast room found, I fear the worst. I'm either too late, too early, or in the wrong place. It's empty.

The first signs of dawn greet me on stepping outside. It's surprisingly chilly. Walking toward the team's supplies truck, the thought of putting my hands into a cold bucket of water to wash down our cars sends chills up my back. Motorola chief mechanic George Noyes is wearing his famous grimace as he tries to stretch a tire onto a rim. And Geoff Brown, another team mechanic, from Canada, stands nearby — apparently happy to watch "how its done."

Greeting them both with the standard "morning," I fling my briefcase into the back of the team car I'll be in for the day — a symbolic gesture akin to "clocking in" at the office.

"You guys ready for breakfast?" I ask, while George inspects his finished work.

"What d'you think? Is the breakfast room open?" he replies.

"Yeah, it is. I checked it out before I came out here," I say, grateful that the breakfast room is indeed open. If it weren't, we would only have to kill time by washing our five and sometimes six team cars. Washing cars in the dark — in the cold and before morning coffee — is just about one of the worst starts to a day that a mechanic's job can offer.

After a traditional French breakfast of coffee that resembles mud and a stale croissant, I excuse myself from the table. The team's soigneurs are already busy preparing breakfast for the riders and making the daily supply of sandwiches for the team.

"Remember. Two PB&Js [peanut-butter-and-jelly sandwiches] for Och — today is a long one!" I yell to the soigneurs as we slip out the door, trying to avoid the standard, gruff "no-custom-sandwiches" reply from the soigneurs. They really hate that, even though Och — Jim Ochowicz, the Motorola team general manager — loves his peanut butter and jelly....

Sticking my hand into a freezing cold bucket of soapy water, I begin the daily car-wash calculation: "Five cars times four days. That's 20 more car washes left for the Tour ... not including today. Not too bad. We'll be into single digits before you know it," I think to myself, recalling that the 18 days already in our wake account for 90 car washes!

Car wash finished, it's off to the kitchen area of Motorola's team truck. It's here where the soigneurs keep most of their supplies. It's also where the two-way radio system, used by the Motorola riders to communicate with Och during the race, is kept.

While others unload the bikes from the back, I quickly inspect the radio to ensure that the batteries are charged. More than once the power in the truck has gone out overnight (for one of many reasons) and left the radio batteries following suit one hour into the race.

For some crazy reason, I foolishly volunteered to father this daily responsibility. And it must be said that since we started working with Motorola to develop a better communication system within the race, I've come to regret that more than a few times.

It's a job that encompasses every ounce of early-morning attention. As the other mechanics unload up to 18 bikes and 10 pairs of spare wheels and prepare them for "airing," I check that the radio is functioning properly before mounting it on Canadian rider Steve Bauer's bike, which carries a transmitter under the saddle. Why Steve and not the others? Simple — he doesn't mind using it as much as they do!

After putting Bauer's bike on the roof of one of the four cars in the Motorola entourage, and then helping the others load the other cars with the remaining bikes and wheels, I realize that it's my turn to ride in the first car today. "No nap today," I mumble to myself dejectedly.

Geoff and I take turns riding in the first car. It's more to give each other a mental break from the stress of being in the No. 1 car than anything else. As for George, he always drives the truck to the next hotel because he suffers from car sickness … or so he says.

As I bend down to pick up some spare wheels, I realize how stiff my back is. At the age of 26, you'd think I shouldn't be having any trouble. But after six or seven hours a day in the back of a race car, three weeks in row, driving on small, twisty, rough, often mountainous roads, you'd think differently.

This being my fourth Tour de France, I begin wondering how I possibly made it this far. But then, how in the hell has a rider like Englishman Sean Yates done 12 of them? It's enough to make me humbly sit in the back of a car — especially when the riders finally arrive from breakfast and interrupt my thoughts of self-pity.

The miles raced are etched in their haggard faces. And their shuffle is akin to that of prisoners on death row — certainly slower than they were walking a couple of weeks ago. The sight of their skeletal bodies and visages, as they get into the team cars bound for today's stage start, fills me with compassion. It's too easy to forget how hard their jobs can be....

The 60km drive over small country roads to the start is long enough for the Motorola riders to reap a little extra rest. And within an instant, the riders in my company are asleep — seemingly undisturbed by my frantic driving to keep up with the other Motorola team cars.

After following the *Départ* signs to the stage start area and arriving there, Geoff and I unload the race bikes. Meanwhile, like condemned souls, the Motorola riders slowly pile out, get their race food and bottles from the soigneurs, and head to the nearby sponsor's village — the hubbub of all pre-stage activity at the Tour. For them, it's a welcome source of social recourse before another day of brutal racing.

While I keep a vigil on the Motorola team cars in case the riders need help with anything, Geoff heads into the tent village to collect some fruit for lunch. It isn't long before I'm summoned.

"Scotty, have you got some grease?" asks Yates from the other side of the car.

"You bet," I answer, reaching into my toolbox for a grease gun. He always needs his pedals greased for freer movement. You'd think I'd beat him to it one of these days.

After attending to several more similar tasks, I am put on alert by the "five-minutes-to-start" whistle, or *appel* as it is known in French. And for another day of punishment, the riders make their way to the start line.

The team's guest for the day is from Motorola France, one of the sponsor's many divisions that have supported us since the multinational electronic giant started backing the team in 1991. He introduces himself, and suddenly Och is back at the car, ready to drive us on the long stage.

"I've got you a *Herald Tribune*. All set to go?" Och asks, handing me the newspaper that is worth its weight in gold for any member of the only American and English-speaking team in Europe.

"Yep, thanks. What did Motorola close at yesterday?" I ask, playing the same little game we do each morning on the Tour.

"Didn't have time to check," Och replies, while preparing to start the car and follow the race entourage out of town and into the French countryside.

Unbeknown to me, the first problem of the day is about to hit us.... Och turns the ignition key. There's no response — except for a rapid clicking sound, which signals a dead car battery.

It's time for quick decisions, the foremost of which is to ensure that our riders aren't stranded without support as we try to sort out our problem. I call on the race radio to our directeur sportif, Hennie Kuiper, a former Dutch professional, who is in the No. 2 car: "Hennie.... Hennie.... We've got a dead battery." I hope he will instinctively move into the No. 1 position and cover the riders while we fix the battery.

Ironically, it was the riders who'd left on the car radio, running the battery down. I recall that this isn't the first time the riders have been guilty. I hate when this happens ... I really do.

Explaining what jumper cables are to a person who doesn't speak your language — nor you his or her language — isn't the easiest thing in the world to do. However, after some creative gestures and my broken French, I finally got the point across to one of the Garde Républicaine motorcyclists. After sensing my urgency, he disappears in haste as if he were answering to the needs of President Jacques Chirac himself. And within a few minutes — and out of breath — he is back, with cables in hand.

Members of the Garde Républicaine — the most elite of France's police forces — are hand-picked for the Tour as a reward for their duties in protecting the French President and visiting dignitaries. They make an impressive support unit for the Tour, and without them, the race would not be the same. One only has to see how they operate to realize the pride they carry in fulfilling their duties — from finding jumper cables for broken-down American team cars, to escorting the yellow jersey wearer and Tour VIPs to and from the race. The Garde executes every task as if the world depended on it.

Nevertheless, there are times when fate simply continues to turn its back on you. And when I returned with the jumper cables, I realized that this was one of those times. Och was fumbling with the hood latch — a repeated hassle with the cars. After a chorus of tight-lipped curses, I ran to the back of the car, found my tool box, and returned with a large screwdriver, with which I managed to pry open the latch. After a quick jump and a hearty "*merci*" to the gendarmes, we finally got aboard to speed off after the departing peloton. But we soon realized it was much farther ahead than expected....

And to think the day had only just started!

Rejoining the race after missing the start is not easy in a team car, despite its having the highest priority accreditation. This is particularly true when the local police have re-opened the course to the public! I called out directions to Och — who could have been mistaken for auditioning as "The Phantom of the Opera," as he thumped his fists on the horn to warn people off the road.

As our speedometer reads 110 kph, and then 120, my palms begin to sweat and my heart races. I know this is one of the most dangerous situations that we can find ourselves in. Once you are out of the race's "rolling enclosure," anything can happen. And until you get back in, you're always pushing your luck. There is no policing, nor a single race marshal to indicate the way. Nobody expects to see a "lost" team car go flying by.

As much as these frustrations can get you down on the Tour, they compare little to the danger that hovers over us like a thunder cloud. That is, to hit an innocent bystander. Most people will have sat on the roadside all morning — and sometimes all night — to get a good view of the race. Many of them are also under the influence of alcohol, their senses often numbed by the speeding rush of race traffic made up of advance press and publicity vehicles, official race and team cars, motorcycle police and photographers, and the riders themselves. The array of "close-call" tales at the end of each day is never-ending.

Getting closer to the race, we start to feel more secure. It's time to call-in to the other team car. "Hennie, you got a copy?" calls Och over the radio. And while all we get back is a broken static message, we now know we are still at least five kilometers away. Our pursuit continues....

Left ... right ... right ... left over a bridge ... through a town ... and past some farms. Then after what seems more like 50km, the back of the race caravan finally comes into view as our car crests the top of a hill, before it disappears once again. Still, we know we're almost there.

The broom wagon pulls a little to the right to let us through. And upon re-entering the caravan, a sigh of relief prevails. Slowly, we make our way through the first row of cars and then wave to Hennie in our No. 2 car to let us take our position again.

There can be peaceful (even dull) parts in a day, too. And the next hour-and-a-half is just that. As time passes by uneventfully, the only hint of action is the task of passing raincoats to a few riders, who fear the looming black clouds ahead forewarn rain. However, as the Tour steers north and away from the storm, even that potential eludes us. Just as suddenly, rain jackets are returned.

"Fifteen minutes," I say, looking at my watch.

"Yep," replies Och. Our guest looks around at me wondering what we're talking about. Fortunately, he speaks a little English and under-stands when I answer his queried look by adding, "Until lunch. We have a rule ... no lunch until 12 o'clock."

"What's on the menu today?" asks Jim.

"Ham," I reply.

"What? No peanut butter and jam?" he cries, glaring at me in the rearview mirror.

"Sorry Jim, I think the soigneurs ran out."

You'd be surprised how hard it is to find good peanut butter in Europe;

it's next to impossible.

After a modest lunch of a ham sandwich and a Coke, I settle back into my book — my third for the Tour. It's not that I'm such a big reader; but being in a team car for six or seven hours a day, the time is there to read. That is, if you don't get car sick. But, then, the silence and boredom of a quiet stage can erupt without a moment's notice.

"Motorola, *roue avant* (front wheel)! Motorola," bellows the voice behind Radio Tour, the official race radio that transmits news of movement within the peloton to the team cars and press. Instinctively, Och punches the accelerator with his foot and passes the cars between him and the peloton. With my book instinctively thrown to the floor and repeating the words "front wheel," I grip the spare wheel with my right hand, while glancing at the front wheel in the back, which is reserved for Sean Yates. Sean doesn't like the standard radial-bladed wheel everyone else uses. So, I look out the windshield to try and spot our rider, to make sure it *isn't* Sean.

"There he is!" I say to Och.

"On the left! … Wait! There's another … and another still!" I yell, realizing that there are three Motorola riders in the back of the peloton with their hands raised in the air. And each may need rapid-fire wheel changes from the one mechanic — me!

Luckily, my fears are extinguished. They're just trying to get the commissaire's attention for the rider who has flatted. Yet, I'm still left with the split-second decision to determine who it is. Finally, one of them falls behind to signal that he is the needy rider. It's our Italian rider, Andrea Peron.

As we speed up to Peron, I open the car door and stand in the doorway to be ready to jump out just before the car stops. It's one of the more calculating tasks of a Tour mechanic's life. Jump out too soon and you can wind-up with a mouth full of dirt. Do it too slowly and you can waste vital seconds.

Thankfully, I hit the ground running, just as Peron comes to a stop and leans over to open his quick release. I grab his wheel as the quick release is opened, and toss it aside to make sure it doesn't roll into the road.

"Take your foot out!" I yell, trying to overcome the noise of the horns and speeding cars. It amazes me that some riders still need to be told to take their foot out of the pedal when a mechanic is changing a wheel. Trying to change a wheel while a rider balances on one foot and holds his bike is not the easiest thing in the world.

Fortunately, on the first attempt, the new wheel slots into place as I put it into the forks, quickly close the skewer shut, dash around Andrea's left side and snatch up the old discarded wheel. He remounts and gets one of his feet in the pedals. Simultaneously, I give him a push, to help him rejoin the pack as quickly as possible.

Trying to catch my breath, I jog back to the car, exchange the old wheel for a new one on the rear roof rack to keep by my side in the car, and give Jim an okay to drive on.

As Och speeds past the long line of team cars to retrieve Motorola's position in the race entourage, Motorola riders Frankie Andreu, Steve Bauer and Steve Swart help pace Peron back up to the race, making the most of the speeding team cars' draft. Amid a fanfare of horn-blowing by Ochowicz to warn other team directors that his riders are coming up between the cars, we follow them around a sharp right turn. Then, suddenly, in front of us is the Banesto team car.... Miraculously, it gives way at the last moment to let our riders follow their own line through the turn. Finally, they are back with the pack.

Soon after we retrieve our position, Jim asks for the fifth time today — and perhaps the 100th time of the Tour — "What else have we got to eat back there?" I give him the standard answer: "The usual Jim ... muesli bars and PowerBars. That's it." Did he really believe that some day I'd pull out a hot fudge sundae?

"Any fruit?" he asks.

"Only the same black banana we've had for the last two days," I reply.

"Any more peanut butter and jelly sandwiches?"

"Nope," I answer, really wondering now whether he's kidding. But I can see by the look on his face that his mind is elsewhere — probably thinking about one of a thousand different things, from trying to find a sponsor and what riders to hire for next year, to whether tonight we'll have a hotel with phone lines that will help him get his computer on-line. Being the general manager of a professional cycling team may look exciting, but behind the glamour is a feast of potentially hair-wrenching duties. These include keeping sponsors happy, and listening to riders — who get paid more in a day than most people earn in a month — complain about the hotels they're staying in. His job is not my idea of fun....

As the Tour passes the "20km to go sign," the speed picks up. Teams with stage-winning aspirations move to the front to get their sprinters in good position for the finale. A few small attacks go off, but they are quickly brought back. The field realizes that, with the peloton moving at 70 kph, it's futile to try and get away again.

For us at Motorola, the scenario is a little depressing, as the team doesn't have a pure sprinter who can mix with the likes of Mario Cipollini. The possibility of our getting the Tour stage win we so desperately need is almost non-existent.

The Tour is the most important race of the year. Almost everything rides on these three weeks in July. And arriving in Paris with nothing to show for their effort is a harsh verdict for the riders, team personnel and management. And especially for the sponsors, who invest more than $5 million a year in the team in the hopes of success.

"Five kilometers to go!" Almost there, almost finished, and I almost manage a smile as I start contemplating an end to the day. That is, until I realize the team faces another transfer from the finish to our hotel. Like everyone, I hate days that require transfers before and after stages. The simple hope for a good hotel is what keeps many going.

"Chute! Chute! [Crash ... crash!] Banesto! Mercatone Uno! Gewiss! ONCE! Motorola!" The race radio awakens my lost sense of thought as it announces teams with riders involved in a crash.

My stomach immediately tightens up and I get a jolt of adrenaline. I see Och stiffen, too. And, frighteningly, the panicked excitement in the race radio voice indicates that this crash is a big one.

Due to the speed riders are hitting in these final kilometers, crashes like this one are the worst. Yet upon hearing news of a spill, there's no time to think. Immediately, I clench my pair of wheels, pinching the tires simultaneously to check they are fully inflated — an old habit learned after once replacing a wheel with one that had deflated from a slow leak while in the car. Instinctively, I make a fast mental replay of where each rider's spare bikes are on the roof rack. Time is so vital for a mechanic ... yet time saved is time wasted if the wrong equipment is given.

Amid the flurry of team cars fighting for position, the Motorola car slows and I open the door and stand up on the doorway to get a better look up the road to see which Motorola riders are in trouble. Simultaneously, I makes sure Och doesn't try to shoot too narrow a gap while I stand in the doorway. It can happen!

Once, a team director ahead of us decided to move up a few more car lengths and pass through too narrow a gap just as we were ready to come through. I was on the doorway, about to service a rider, when I suddenly saw him ahead. Thankfully, I dove back in just before the wheels in my hand were crushed in the door when it hit the other car! I only just barely got my right leg back in, never mind almost having my body crushed and face smashed into the race-ready rack of the other car.

Now, while standing atop the doorway, the image of the stricken Motorola rider — Lance Armstrong — becomes clear. "It's Lance!" I yell to Och through the open window of the front passenger door. I can't see if Armstrong is badly injured or not; nor what mechanical needs he has. Does he need a new wheel or two? Does he need a new bike? In the few seconds left, I must decide what to do — to run up with just a pair of wheels and change them, or grab the Texan star's spare bike from the rack and run the risk of wasting precious seconds if he doesn't need it.

Straining to spot his bike just before we stop, I see it lying on the ground in a twisted heap, telling me that there was only one thing to do....

The next moments stand as a reminder of the hazards of running to a rider between the team cars in front. Taking the straightest possible line through the maze of opening car doors and mechanics and team directors jumping from them, the fear of suddenly running into them becomes very real. But just as one such thought enters your head, another replaces it. And at this moment, Lance's plight deserves greater concern. In making my way closer to him, it's clear that he's in pretty bad shape.

Putting the bike down in front of him, I try to give him some encouragement. "Come on Lance, let's go! Only a few more kilometers. You can do it! Come on!" But he's in a lot of pain, bleeding from several places and limping. His knee looks pretty bad. Then he appears to be on the verge of sitting down. Some riders sit down and never get back up. And I begin to wonder if this is the beginning of the end of Lance's Tour.

"Come on buddy, you can do it, let's go!" I say, wondering if he's going to tell me where to go instead! He slowly puts his leg over the saddle. And just as slowly I push him through the debris, making sure he's watching where he's going. Picking up speed, giving him words of encouragement, I'm still uncertain if he can even hear me — right up until my final and desperate shove.

After running back, grabbing his mangled bike and throwing it onto the roof rack, I see that Och's concern is just as pained.

"How is he?!" asks Och, once again laying on the horn and punching the accelerator to rejoin the race.

"Not too good." I reply. "He's pretty messed up … hurt his knee."

As we slow and approach Lance, who is riding alone, it's obvious that he's in bad shape. He can barely pedal.

"Are you all right?" Jim yells through the window. Lance just shakes his head.

Then, picking up the radio, Och says, "Hennie. You got a copy? Come up and cover Lance. We're going forward to tell a few of the guys to stop and help Lance!"

One-hundred-twenty kph … 130 … the Motorola car's speed rises. We are far behind the race. But as we approach an underpass, I spot a figure standing in the shadows on the left side, which is also the wrong side to service riders. He's holding a bike. It's Sean Yates!

"Jim! It's Sean….!" is all I manage to get out as Och spots him and slams down on the breaks, throwing me into the back of the front seat and our Fiat into a four-wheel skid from 130 to 0 kph in 50 feet!

Stopping about six meters past Sean, I jump out with a pair of wheels and begin to run across the street, while looking back to make sure no other cars traveling at 130 kph are coming. Then, reaching Sean in the middle of the road, I ask, "What's wrong Sean?" as I grab his bike and carry it to the side of the road.

"Front wheel," he says … and, amazingly, with a sheepish smile. I can't figure out why, but I put in a good wheel to replace one with four or five broken spokes, and push him off. He must have got the wheel caught in someone's pedal or back wheel.

"Okay, Jim!" Och accelerates again, but not for long. After a few seconds, we see two more Motorola riders in the distance. They are barely pedaling, waiting and looking for their teammates. It's Swart and Bauer.

"You guys wait! Sean and Lance are behind!" Och yells out the window. We get a nod in reply as we blast off again.

Up ahead, the remainder of the team cars hover behind the peloton. Two more Motorola riders are hanging back, wondering if they should help out. Och tells them not to wait, and with those words, they immediately get out of the saddle and make a mad sprint to rejoin the field — now racing toward the sprint finish. Then, the same as every day, we are directed away from the finishing straight, to a nearby parking lot.

"Shot, you got a copy?" Och calls into the radio.

"Comeback, Jim," replies John "Shot" Hendershot, the team's head soigneur, who is waiting to attend to our riders at the finish line.

"Where are you parked, Shot?" asks Och, as we attempt to locate our other team cars through the mayhem of the finish area. The crowd is thick, and Och, tooting the horn, clears a way through the mob of fans, who form a wall in front of us.

"Whack!" The passenger-side rearview mirror bends back as it hits a spectator who has moved a little too close. Now we know why European cars have folding mirrors!

"Take the directors' deviation all the way, until you see the Polti team bus and we're on the left side, 100 meters past them," says Shot.

"Okay, Lance was in a crash four kilometers from the finish, and Yates, Bauer and Swart are waiting for him. We don't know how bad he is, but he hit his knee pretty hard."

"All right Jim, Max (the team doctor) is at the finish, and he'll get him cleaned up in the camper when he gets in."

"Ten-four."

We squeeze the team car just behind the Motorola camper van. I curse to myself. The soigneurs' cars are in front of the camper and so I won't be able to watch our race car while I'm loading the bikes on the soigneurs' cars. Neither is Geoff Brown nearby to help out. Still, I don't waste any time. Leaving the car for Och to look after, I jump out and make my way through the dense crowd and past the camper van. I grab the bike from one of our riders who has already finished.

Then comes another bike count, one of about 20 mandatory counts in a day, to make sure nothing is missing, forgotten or even stolen. Life is just one constant count for mechanics, and having a bike stolen is every mechanic's nightmare.

While loading one of the last bikes, press photographers and reporters arrive in droves, obviously having heard about Lance's crash and anxious for his arrival — to get a few "bloody" shots, or a few juicy quotes. Given his condition, that seems doubtful today....

A television crew from the American ABC Sports approaches me and fires a few questions about Lance's condition. You never get used to this. And it always happens when you aren't ready for it. My stomach clenches immediately, and my palms start sweating. I do my best at answering questions about how hurt he is, will he be able to continue tomorrow, and if he needed help getting back on his bike....

The questions went on as I simply made a blubbering fool out of myself

reverse roles

We were in the second team car during a stage of the 1993 Tour de France when I was asked by Jim Ochowicz to drive the car. Jim was never really keen on that idea, as opposed to Hennie Kuiper, and I never knew why. Perhaps Och was worried that if something happened, he would be liable? Certainly, driving a team car is a dangerous thing to do — and to do it for six or seven hours a day for 23 days in a row takes a lot out of you.

Anyway, on this day, Jim did ask me to drive, much to my surprise. I had asked so many times in the past and he always said no; but here we were, pulling over and swapping seats. I was finally driving.

After 20 minutes, Hennie called on the radio from the No. 1 car, closest to the peloton. He had run out of Extran — a carbohydrate drink — and one of our Belgian riders, Michel Dernies, was calling for some. So we obliged and drove up from our 50th position to deliver it.

Simultaneously, several attacks went off the front, the race pace quickened and everything got hectic. We gave Michel the Extran, thinking that would be it and we would drop back to our place behind the race; but then Radio Tour said Frankie Andreu had punctured.

You are only allowed one car near the front and we had two, so because we were closer to the front Hennie dropped back. Then I realized that I — the mechanic who is meant to change the wheel — was behind the wheel driving!

I told Jim he had to change the wheel. He said, "No … no … get Hennie back.

I'm not changing a wheel." In those conditions, it would be hard for me to change the wheel. It's too dangerous for the driver to get out, because he would get out on the side where other team cars pass. With the race speed at 65 kph, it wasn't me who was going to change wheels. Jim wanted Hennie to come back up, but he had stopped for a natural break and said he couldn't get back in time. So Jim had to do it. Then, as this discussion was taking place, Frankie was wondering why we were being so indecisive, and he started yelling at us.

Jim finally got out and ran up to Frankie … in a real panic, too! Then, when Frankie got off his bike, waiting for the change to be completed, Jim got Frankie's chain caught up. That I can understand, considering he was in a pressured situation doing a job that was not normally his to do. But I still couldn't get out and help, because of the traffic.

I just sat there, watching Jim having a terrible time. Frankie was trying to stay calm, looking at me look at Jim. Then Neil Lacey, another Motorola mechanic, arrived with Hennie and pushed Jim out of the way, fixed Frankie's wheel and pushed him off.

Jim was still in shock. He grabbed the wheels and tried to put the old wheel on the rear rack. Realizing it was full, he ran to the front but couldn't reach high enough. Then, he suddenly jumped on the hood! There I was, looking up through the windshield, laughing, not quite believing what was happening!

Jim finally got in the car. I kept laughing while we quickly switched places. I never drove the team car again. ⊁━C

… stuttering and stammering, trying to find the words for my one spot in the limelight. All I hope is that my part will get edited out, or that no one will be watching back home if it isn't.

Lance and the riders with him roll up. Predictably, the press immediately goes into a feeding frenzy, trying to get their shots; but the riders are one step ahead and jump in the camper van first, allowing Max to take a look at Lance, clean him up and drive off to the hotel as quickly as possible.

We hit the *autoroute* without error. But, after a few minutes, that respite starts to fade when someone driving one of our other cars comes across the radio, saying: "Hennie, if we take the next exit it looks a little shorter to the hotel."

"I asked at the start, and a cop told me they're about the same, but that road you're talking about has more traffic this time of day. So I think this one is better," replies Hennie.

"I don't know, Hennie. This road here looks a lot shorter to me on my map, I think we should take it."

"I don't think so. This one's better."

Clearly, emotions are starting to rise. And I hope to myself that one or the other will stop pushing their case before somebody gets really pissed off. And if they do, it can stress out the riders, which is what we're trying to avoid in the first place.

Alas, the signal light of the car behind me flashes in my rearview mirror and soon after come the words: "I'm taking this road, see you all at the hotel." It wasn't Hennie. Rule No. 1? Always stick together!

I still decide to put in my two cents' worth. "Let's stick together. Hennie's the director, let him direct!" I say, reminding myself and him that that is his job, after all.

We finally do stick together. And after what seems like the really long way, the hotel is found on a small side street and in a obscure part of town. Ironically, we probably would have arrived a lot earlier if we had followed the alternate directions most of us opposed.

The hotel area doesn't provide ideal working conditions. Nevertheless, the summer weather motivates me to start washing bikes immediately, while George and Geoff unload the team cars. Between the three of us, we switch work routines every day.

"How was it?" asks George, greeting us with the standard post-stage question.

"Not too bad," I reply with a weathered tone.

It's hard to be enthusiastic by now. I've been stuck in a car for almost nine hours, a little more than average. It's 6:15 p.m., and there's still a lot of work ahead. I'm hungry, tired and looking forward to Paris.

While I give George a run-down of the day's highs — and lows — a team car carrying Lance and Max pulls out of the parking lot. As it disappears out of view, we look at each other with sad and disappointed expressions. Sensing they are en route for the hospital, where Armstrong will have some X-rays, I figure our shot at a stage win has been blown.

After the bikes are washed, I immediately start work on repairing Armstrong's bike. After a thorough inspection, the frame appears to have escaped serious damage from the crash — unlike every other piece, which needs replacing. If only the frame had been ruined, then I could simply pull out Armstrong's brand new spare race bike. However, we only replace bikes if absolutely necessary.

Following the resurrection of Lance's bike, it looks as good as new, especially after touching up the scratched paintwork. Meanwhile, after finishing their own tasks, George and Geoff work on the two other bikes I was meant to have checked. Finally, after stowing all the gear for the night — from the first bike to the last hose — we breathe a sigh of relief. I close the back door of the truck, and George sets the alarm. It's time to start appreciating the work done.

"Good job, guys," I say, while walking to the hotel lobby. "One more down. How many to go?"

Everyone knows how many stages to go, but we try not to remind ourselves. Still, it's a good feeling to finish another stage and know you've done a good job as a crew. It's remarkable how important and critical it is to work efficiently together as a team of mechanics. As with bike riders, if you work well together, you're going to do a better job.

George and I have worked together for almost four years. When you work with someone that long, it makes a big difference. We never discuss who's going to do what, or how we should do things. We instinctively know not to waste time and effort figuring things out. As a result, you concentrate more on the job at hand that, for us, is making sure each bike is prepared and ready for the next day. Working with someone new takes much more time and effort, and can distract you from the duties at hand.

After a quick shower, it's time for dinner. By the time I arrive at the table, except for a few members of the team staff, almost everyone is finished. Tonight's special is a plate of the "finest" in French cuisine — a tough steak with the thickness and consistency of a worn Vittoria Corsa CX tire and boiled spinach, which is cold by now. After a few bites, I'm already asking the waiter for some cheese — for me, one of the few redeeming qualities of France.

We talk for a while, and gradually numbers at the table dwindle as people retire or take care of the last responsibilities of the day. However, whether it's sending a fax to the office or a sponsor, seeing to the riders' needs, or simply checking your laundry, people's minds are already fixed on getting ready for the awaiting day.

"Seven o'clock?" I ask George, double checking our time to meet for breakfast.

"Sounds good…. Good night," he replies.

"Good night," I answer, thinking "good idea," as well, as I look at my watch, which reads 11 p.m. — time for a short read before sleeping. But then, that choice is stifled as soon as I open my door. Serge, my roommate, is already sound asleep. With reading out of the question, I set my alarm for 6:30 a.m. and put my head on the pillow, realizing how tired I really am.

"Four more days to go," I think to myself, trying to look forward to the few days off I'll have after the Tour is over.

I'm going to need those days as much as this sleep.

chapter two

On the Road Again

For a first-time arrival at the Motorola team's Belgian headquarters — at Kerkstraat 1 in the West Flanders town of Harelbeke — everything appeared so big and busy. The atmosphere was totally different from what I had experienced with the U.S.-based Coors Light team. It was almost unfriendly, with everyone so businesslike and seemingly having no time to help me or explain things.

Arriving in Brussels after an 18-hour trip from the United States, I was immediately put to work. Sure, when asked if I wanted to start work, I immediately agreed. Wouldn't most people on their first day of a new and much-sought-after job?

But after a while, it became clear that this unfriendly attitude reflected everyone's constant preoccupation of fulfilling their tasks on a major league professional cycling team. It was hard to adapt to.

It's not that Coors Light and other U.S.-based teams are "fun houses," but they are more akin to a family when compared to a Motorola. Racing in the U.S. is much less frequent and easier, so there is always enough time to do things. People just don't have the time or energy to expend on things that aren't necessary.

Going from what one thinks is a big team (Coors Light) and believing one knows everything, to starting with a giant team (Motorola) in another part of the world, and realizing you know barely anything, is a huge chasm to cross.

My first year on the Motorola squad in 1992 was very difficult. By the end of 1993, I thought I was an old hand; but when January 3 came around — with a New Year's Eve hangover still lingering — it sure seemed early to be returning to Europe for the 1994 season. Every year, each winter vacation seemed to be a little bit shorter. It probably felt that way because in my first two years with Motorola, we didn't leave for Europe until after our training camp in California. This year, the camp was in Italy.

Staying in the U.S. until late January made it feel like work really hadn't begun. And by the time we did fly back to Belgium, the anxiety of arriving back in Europe was shared by the entire team.

A NEW SEASON

Each part of the season is different, and the beginning is especially so, because it's the time when everyone on the team is excited. There's the excitement of seeing one another and sharing holiday stories after two months apart ... and the anticipation of a new season. Every year, we believed that we had a better team than the year before — better riders, equipment, staff, vehicles and race schedule. We felt we were invincible.

For the staff, it's a hectic rush to get everything ready for the first road trip. The soigneurs are busy loading the supplies truck with food, drinks, medicine and massage products. Although, as the majority of their work is with the riders on the road, they tend to be less occupied beforehand. Our job is mostly focused on preparation of equipment. It's a constant race to build bikes and wheels, glue tires, order more equipment, and stay on top of inventory. No matter how early the season starts, there is always an incredible amount of work to do upon arrival in Europe.

Normally, there are at least 30 to 40 bikes to build — a race bike and spare for each rider. Then we need to build a pair of training wheels for each rider and at least 25 pairs of race wheels for each truck, totaling 140 wheels. But that isn't all. Other early-season tasks include preparing the team cars and trucks, working with the rack builder to design and install new roof racks and various types of radios in them, liaising with team sponsors, and loading the truck with spare equipment and tools.

Fortunately, the Motorola team rarely changed equipment suppliers. Changing them only creates extra work and makes you consider an early retirement. By staying with the same bike manufacturer, a lot of bikes can be held over from the previous year, and used as spares. If component suppliers don't change, parts from the previous year that were still in good shape can still be used. Thankfully, wheels can be retained, unless the rim sponsor changes. Rebuilding all the wheels takes a huge amount of time.

Once all the bikes are built, the riders' positions are then set. And, if they haven't made any changes over the winter, they can ride them straight away. However, regular position checks are still made during the season. This facilitates the preparation of duplicate spare bikes, or ensures that the riders' positions don't alter.

In 1994, Motorola signed up Volvo as a cosponsor and so received new cars and trucks. It was great to have such high-quality vehicles to work with — probably the single most important difference in any of the improvements that we had in all my years in professional cycling. It improved our overall image as a professional team and made work for the staff much more efficient and pleasant.

Once the trucks were prepared and loaded, the annual pre-season training camp beckoned us; and, until 1994, that meant a trip to Santa Rosa, California — a fun location with plenty of things to do and see. There were movies to go to, a wide variety of restaurants, and a maze of malls to shop in — amenities we would soon miss during the long European season.

The only problem with Santa Rosa was the cold, and often rainy, weather at that time of year. Also, most of the riders on the team lived in Europe. By the time they got over the jet lag, it was almost time to turn around and go back to Europe. And all this for bad weather? It didn't add up.

For mechanics, training camp is a lot of sudden rushes ... and then waits. We are either busy preparing the bikes, or sitting around waiting for the riders to return from training — and then cleaning the bikes and putting them away.

There is also a lot of one-on-one work with the riders, helping with any mechanical problems. Many riders use the off-season to experiment with equipment. So quite a bit of time at camp is spent measuring, comparing, adjusting and changing handlebars, stems, cranks, saddles and any new products, and then varying positions.

One evening as I was closing the truck for the day at our 1994 training camp, Andy Hampsten came out and asked if I could help him with his bike. He said the position didn't feel right on his new bike.

I measured Andy's bike, asked him if he had made any position changes in the off-season, and with my own notes showed him that his new bike's measurements matched those from the previous fall. This didn't convince Andy — which is usually the case — and he asked for a plumb bob and tape measure. The tape measure was no problem, but I hadn't used a plumb bob for years, so I put one together for him using some dental floss and a crank bolt.

Even though I was a little irritated that he was dismissing my very accurate measurements for a plumb bob's, I was pretty curious as to what he had in mind. Sometimes you have to humor these guys.

Andy put on his shoes and sat on his bike leaning against a wall. With the crankarm horizontal, he wanted to drop the plum bob from the front of his knee and compare how it lined up at the pedal spindle. I was a little surprised. I hadn't seen anyone do this since my old days at the bike shop. It's a well-known and reliable method, but I expected Andy would have had a more scientific method up his sleeves. Still, I obligingly knelt down and measured the distance the string was behind the spindle for him; and after doing this a few times from both sides he seemed convinced that our measurement was accurate and that his position was where it should be.

He knew what his position should be. No matter what method Andy used, he showed he knew what saddle positions should be. I was impressed.

OFF TO THE RACES

Once training camp was finished and the Motorola team was back at team headquarters in Belgium, there was never much time to get everything ready for the first racing trip of the year. There were still positions to adjust on the riders' spare; the team trucks had to be loaded; and an ever-present list of last-minute tasks had to be taken care of.

Motorola usually had a double program, with two separate parts of the team racing in different locations at the same time. This ensured that all of the riders got enough racing to stay in good form. Some larger teams like Mapei-GB — which had almost 30 riders in 1995 — follow three programs throughout the year. And although Mapei-GB is registered in Italy, its tentacles also spread to Spain and Belgium. How the team stayed organized amazed the other mechanics. Just distributing equipment for a team the size of Motorola was already enough of a logistical nightmare.

For us, the most important races — besides the Tour de France, Giro d'Italia, Vuelta a España and Tour DuPont — were the one-day World Cup races. There are 10 or 11 such races each year, with the most prestigious being the spring classics Milan-San Remo, the Tour of Flanders, Paris-Roubaix and Liège-Bastogne-Liège.

The spring classics are not only important for the sponsors, they also set the mood within a team for the rest of the season and are critical for teams looking to renew or find a new sponsor for the following year.

The classics are "monuments" of the sport, with each event having its own character, heritage and terrain. Winning just one of them gives a rider as much honor and prestige as winning an Olympic gold medal or world title.

FEBRUARY

As February dawns, so too does the anticipation of the first races. There is a feverish excitement of finally getting things underway, after spending so long in the preparatory phase of the season. Unsurprisingly, the riders are also anxious to see if their off-season training — or lack of it — will show itself.

Until recent years, the events in February were regarded as training races. They provided a platform for riders to get into shape for the spring classics, and weren't as difficult or as important to win as they are now.

However, with every race now allocated points for the UCI world rankings, even results from these season-openers have become important. Instead of beginning the season with, say, less than 3000km of training in their legs, most cyclists start the year with up to 10,000km. Some begin the season with as many as 13,000km! They simply want to be in their best condition early and pull off as many top results as possible. As a consequence, riders short on winter kilometers now find that these once enjoyable early-season events are some of the toughest of the whole year.

Motorola's season always began with a two-day haul by car to the south of Spain for the five-day Ruta del Sol stage race. After that, we headed north to the south of France for the five-day Mediterranean Tour. Then, another team truck and squad of personnel would travel down from Belgium and meet us in France, for a transfer of equipment and bikes, and a replenishment of food and drinks. From here, one part of the team headed to the one-day Trofeo Laigueglia race, just over the border in Italy, before taking a 24-hour ferry trip south from Genoa to Sicily, for the Tour of Sicily. The other part of the squad returned to Belgium for the Het Volk and Kuurne-Brussels-Kuurne semi-classics.

It was at the 1992 Laigueglia race and Tour of Sicily that I made my on-road debut with Motorola. It didn't start auspiciously....

After Laigueglia, two soigneurs and I arrived in Genoa for the boat trip to Sicily. We had plenty of time to find our way to the port. But after driving around like madmen for two hours, asking directions and only get more and more lost, we still hadn't found the boat. Finally, with 10 minutes to go, we waved down a police car and Serge Borlée — one of the soigneurs who is a full-time Brussels policeman — jumped out of the car and flashed his police badge at the carabinieri. Serge explained our predicament in French and broken Italian to the police, and in moments their siren was on and they were giving us a high-speed police escort through downtown Genoa.

Then, after negotiating a maze of turns into the harbor area, we saw a bunch of local Italian teams waiting in line for the boat. The vehicles were about to embark, when our police friends stopped and had a few words with the ferry officials. In moments, after giving the police a supply of team caps and memorabilia — and a hearty *grazie* — we found ourselves the first ones on the boat! But getting lost on the way to the port was just the first of our problems….

It didn't take long to realize that our ferry ride was going to be "the boat trip from hell." The ship was designed for trucks transporting produce to and from Sicily, and its restaurant and bar were both closed that night. After a rough night at sea, I woke up feeling a little seasick, yet still anxious for breakfast to put something in my stomach — although bad coffee and a stale croissant wasn't exactly what I had in mind. Being surrounded by burly, mean-looking Sicilian truck drivers didn't help my mood.

However, I was still determined to show my independence — whether trying to speak Italian or French. Pointing to a guy who looked like he was nursing a mean hangover behind the counter while selling coffee and croissants, I asked Serge and our other French soigneur, James, "Do you know how to ask for more croissants? That guy speaks a little French doesn't he?"

"Yeah, just say, '*As-tu des croissants, connard?*'" replied James. Knowing a little French myself, I figured out the first part easily but asked James, "What does *connard* mean?"

"It is a way of being polite, like saying sir," said James encouragingly. But soon after my parrot repetition of his words, the vendor quickly grew angry.

It was clear that something had upset him. His shoulders tightened , his face turned red, and he said nothing in reply … much to my surprise. Thinking he simply misunderstood, I decided to give it another try.

"*As-tu des crois….*" I managed to say, before being interrupted by a chorus of laughter behind me. Turning, I saw Serge and James doubled over.

"What the heck does *connard* mean?!" I demanded from James and Serge. But they couldn't stop laughing. Then, between gasps for air, Serge said: "*Connard* means asshole in French!" — which forced them to break into another laughing fit. I must have turned white as a sheet. Certainly, my enthusiasm for learning French was never quite the same after that incident.

We finally docked in Palermo after midnight, and under sheets of pouring rain, with me in one car and my new colleagues in the other, we drove away from the harbor. I asked the two soigneurs by radio for directions to our hotel. But after a few seconds came the reply I would learn to dread on every road trip: "I don't know."

I was surprised that not only did these guys have no idea where the hotel was, but they hadn't even thought to get directions.

After a few minutes of vainly trying to discuss our next move and getting only static radio response in reply, I realized that they were just toying with me. And it wasn't going to stop there....

As they started driving faster and faster, up to 100 kph through red lights and blind intersections. They were trying to lose me! I couldn't believe it! What had I done to get myself in such a mess?

Asking them to slow down, they only responded by speeding up. I was terrified, my heart was racing, and my knuckles were white on the wheel. What would I do if I lost these guys? What would any newcomer do in a place renowned for its gangsters and violence where I couldn't even speak the language at 1 o'clock in the morning, in pouring rain?

And, foolishly, I had left my bag with maps, race information and the name of the hotel in the other car! I began to panic, but then realized that the speeding car was heading out of town instead of going in circles. For me, this was the first clue that they knew exactly where they were going. Or so I thought....

After a few miles, we started heading up a mountain. Then, under pouring rain that limited our visibility, the speed picked up again. The feeling returned that they actually didn't know where they were going.

"Do you guys know where you are going?" I called into the radio, hoping they would answer me. And they did, although not with the response I expected: "I think the hotel is near the airport. When we get to the top of the mountain we will be able to see the planes landing and then we'll know where the airport is." I could hear laughing in the background.

That was it. They were still joking around! I couldn't believe it. "If we do find the airport, I'm on the first flight back to the States," was all I could think.

After finally turning around and heading back down the mountain, their pace was once again impossible to follow. My car started acting funny, as if it were going to spin out on every turn. And I was still losing ground on them. Then, almost at the bottom and with only a couple more turns left, my hands suddenly tightened on the wheel. I felt the back end swing out, and immediately I turned the wheel to try and correct the slide. All I could do was hope this maneuver wasn't too late.

As the car straightened out, I finally took a breath, not realizing that until then I had been holding my breath the whole time. I slowed the car considerably, watching the other car disappear out of sight. It all came to me then. Very rarely have I been struck by such an eye-opening experience. I suddenly realized how stupid I had been in getting so nervous and excited, risking my life and almost crashing the team car. For what purpose? Just so I could keep up with these two? That was pretty ridiculous.

What was the worst that could have happened had I gone slower? I could have slept in the car, or found a hotel in town and tried to find the team hotel in the morning. It would have been the others who would have been in trouble for abandoning me in the middle of nowhere.

Then, after calming down and pulling off to the side of the road, I soon realized what my real problem was: a flat tire. As I unloaded stuff from the back of the car into the pouring rain, I reminded myself that things could be worse. After pulling out the spare wheel and locating the jack and lug wrench in the dark, I began to change the tire — even laughing at myself while jumping up and down on the lug wrench to loosen the seized bolts. This would be no 10-second wheel change!

After a time, headlights appeared from the direction I had just come from. I hoped the driver would see me. The only other option was that I would be run over. Finally, the car slowed and came to a stop. Blinded by the lights I put my hand up to shield my eyes. In vain. I couldn't see a thing. I heard yelling from behind the lights, but it was barely audible over the sound of heavy rain. Caution prevailed as I approached the car. Thankfully, it was the police. What they were doing on a desolate country road at 2 a.m. I will never know; but thank God they were there.

After my verbal fumble in Italian, they eventually understood that I was here for the Tour of Sicily, and helped by shining their lights on me while I finished changing the tire. Then, with the job nearly done, my "lost" soigneurs, who had seemingly abandoned me, suddenly appeared!

"Where have you been? We lost you," yelled James over the thunderous rain, suddenly seeming so concerned with my well-being.

"What does it look like?!" I responded, my good mood long gone and body shivering in the rain like a leaf. Their return meant little now. Meanwhile, Serge, who was talking to the police, had the day's first bit of good news: "They're going to show us where the hotel is!"

After following the police for miles through the countryside, I began wondering if even they knew where they were going. However, when we finally pulled up to our hotel, I realized that we never ever would have found this place without them. The carabinieri had rescued us again — twice in two days.

I learned a lot on that trip to Sicily, most importantly to always be self-sufficient and well informed. After that episode, I always carried my own maps and race/hotel information with me. I tried to make a habit of always knowing what was going on and where I was going.

That first Tour of Sicily was my initiation into the world of European cycling, but the lessons didn't end there. The boat trip and hair-raising car trip to my hotel was only the beginning. Food poisoning left me bedridden for three days. And after the race, I had to drive overnight to Belgium in order to get back in time for another race.

MARCH

With March come the first really important races of the year. The amnesty period for riders to find their racing legs and get into "racing shape" is over and the team bosses accept few excuses for a poor performance.

Making what is called the A-team is vital for every rider at this time of year. It not only shows the team's directeur sportif and personnel that a rider has

been diligent with training, diet and rest during the winter, but also determines a rider's seasonal program. Riders on form find it a lot easier to stay in
the A-team than riders short of condition fighting their way up from the B-
team. The second-string squad is often left contesting small, little-known events.

The first two weeks of March include the Tour of Murcia in Spain,
Paris-Nice in France and Tirreno-Adriatico in Italy — all multi-day stage
races — which lead up to the first major one-day World Cup classic:
Milan-San Remo in Italy.

Of the three stage races, Paris-Nice and Tirreno-Adriatico are the most
important. They are the first "category one" stage races of the year.

There is often heated debate about which of them is the hardest and best
preparatory event for Milan-San Remo. Many feel that with Italy being the
dominant nation in contemporary cycling, Tirreno-Adriatico is not just one
of the hardest races of the spring but of the entire year. It also attracts a lot
of publicity because it finishes just two days before Milan-San Remo,
while Paris-Nice ends a week before.

The importance of Milan-San Remo itself is unquestioned. However,
it always struck me as odd that the team would give riders new titanium bikes
for Paris-Nice and Tirreno-Adriatico. It seemed too early in the season.
But each year, our duty of handing out such top-of-the-range equipment came
earlier and earlier. Years ago, riders would only get light bikes for the Tour
de France. Then the hand-out would begin at the Tour DuPont in May. And
by 1994, it was the beginning of March.

Still, we always tried to save something special for the really big races —
including Milan-San Remo. The riders are really under pressure to perform
in the World Cup classics. And with Milan-San Remo being their first for the
year, it always provided a psychological boost to give them new titanium
gears or parts, fancy wheels or light bikes. Every little bit counted. It helped
the riders to know that the staff was putting in an extra effort for them.

So, when we were back on the road for another season, the arrival of
Milan-San Remo meant it was time for that "little extra effort."

chapter three

The Spring Classics

Next to the major national tours — the Tour de France, Giro d'Italia and Vuelta a España — the single-day World Cup classics are the most prestigious races to win. And the very first of those classics, Milan-San Remo in Italy, is one of the biggest. Every Italian cyclist dreams of winning this race, which was founded in 1907 and has been held every year since, except for 1916 and 1944. Those Italians who do win become instant national heroes. And those *stranieri*, or foreigners, who take the honors in San Remo are often labeled as the enemy — especially if their win has come at the cost of an Italian victory.

The race's importance is also underlined by its timing. Known as the Primavera — the first of spring — Milan-San Remo attracts a feast of publicity. Not only is it the first major classic of the year, it is also very much a celebration of the new season. In most Anglo-Saxon countries like the U.S., Australia and Great Britain, it's hard to understand why cycling is so popular in western Europe. One of the main reasons is the sport's tradition. Some classics have been going on for a hundred years, usually taking almost the exact same route since they were founded.

Small towns through which these races pass often shut down completely for the event. For many of the towns, the passage of a bike race is the most exciting thing that happens all year. And for anyone working on a race, it's incredible to speed through a small European town, to see and hear the thousands of spectators lining the street. Many have been watching these races go past since they were children.

Cycling is also unique because you can get right up close to the athletes at the start or finish, meet and talk with them, or get an autograph if you're determined enough. What other sports allow such proximity to the stars? Cycling is a sport for the people, with no need for a ticket. If you want to see the event … just go.

Milan-San Remo starts at the Piazza Duomo in central Milan, one of Italy's most popular tourist attractions. Funnily enough, it took me three editions of the race before I noticed the duomo, or cathedral, despite having stood next to it for more than an hour each year while preparing our team bikes. I was just too busy keeping an eye on all our equipment, I guess!

The race start is the most chaotic in cycling, with tens of thousands of people swarming around the team cars, unprotected by any barriers or crowd control. To keep a better eye on the bikes, I would keep them on the car racks until the very last minute. I've been very fortunate to have never had a bike stolen.

There have been some close calls, however. After a stage finish at the Nissan Classic in Ireland one year, while watching the car, I asked someone to stop touching one of the wheels on the rack. He was trying to undo the quick release. Incredibly, he completely ignored me. On such occasions, people usually stop touching something when asked. Then, as I walked up to the guy to make sure he wasn't going to walk off with the wheel, he suddenly turned on me. In an instant I realized the whole thing was a ploy to draw me into a fight, so his mates now circling the car could clean it out.

To say it was a precarious moment is an understatement. I was in a crowd of thousands of people, with no police in sight, and this gang waiting to pounce with no fear of being caught. Fortunately, some sweet talking stubbed out their criminal intent: I gave them a bunch of team hats and posters and, lying through my teeth, said I would give them all autographs of the riders if they came to the hotel that night.

After Milan-San Remo, with everything packed up and ready to go, George Noyes and I continued on to Spain for the Setmana Catalana — a five-day stage race that is the last stop of this season-opening road trip. After that, it was back to Belgium for the toughest and most grueling races of the year, the April classics!

The first major lead-up, the Three Days of De Panne in Belgium, is also known by many as the Three Days of Pain. Because of the frequently bad weather and tough cobblestone courses, it's one of the hardest stage races of the year to finish, even though it's only three days long!

One wonders if there are any riders who actually enjoy doing De Panne. But it is a necessity for riders wanting to do well in the famous Tour of Flanders, the first of the northern classics and the second round of the World Cup after Milan-San Remo.

Unsurprisingly, most riders are very nervous about the few weeks that follow De Panne; and for a couple of reasons. They know how important it is for them and their teams to get good results. And more importantly, they know how difficult these races are and how much suffering is involved to get those results. There is no faking it in the April classics.

The worst conditions I've ever worked in were at the 1995 Three Days of De Panne. At our hotel on the morning of stage one, it was bitingly cold, and all our cars in the parking lot had frost and ice caked on them. George and I unloaded the bikes from the truck as usual and proceeded to load the cars and get everything ready for the race. It was so cold that the right leg of my bike stand snapped while I was tightening the pedal of a bike mounted in it. Fortunately, the race start was near the Motorola team headquarters, so we drove there to arrange for a new stand for the rest of the race. Easier said than done....

Once we arrived at the team office with all the riders, I went about my business of unloading bikes from the car and getting ready for the start. It was snowing, and we must have loaded and unloaded the bikes from the car three or four times while our directeur sportif tried to decide if the riders should cycle to the start four kilometers away or go by car. Finally, in our haste to leave, I forgot to take the new bike stand.

In the snow, rain and freezing temperatures, I was busy the entire day. Fortunately, I didn't have to get out of the car too often. My main tasks were handing up dry clothes, trying to dry wet clothes in the back of the car, preparing and handing up warm tea and food, and tightening up brakes on the riders' bikes. But with the race splitting up right from the start — as is often the case in wet weather — it was still hard to service all our riders in the different groups.

Brakes are the greatest casualty of days like that. A rider can go through an entire set of new brake pads, to the point of wearing out all the rubber and finally riding on the metal shoe itself! While some riders stopped to tighten their brakes themselves, many were so cold that they couldn't. When they were lucky, I was able to do it by leaning out the window from the team car. Nevertheless, by the end of the stage some riders were way off the back after stopping so many times.

The snow intensified as the day wore on, falling its hardest while I waited at the showers for riders to arrive after the finish. Grabbing a rain cap from the directeur sportif's rain bag and putting it on to try and keep my already soaked head warm, I realized my work was just beginning. The next few hours were spent trying to keep warm while working on the bikes.

I loaded the bikes one by one as our riders sporadically arrived, battered and beaten like veterans from a war. Finally, everyone had arrived except for Italian Andrea Peron who, I thought, had retired to the broom wagon. Then, upon hearing a distant yell, I looked up to see where it was coming from. A rider was hurtling down the slight downhill stretch toward the team cars. I didn't recognize who it was because of the mud and dirt covering him from head to toe. Only a thick Italian-accented cry gave a clue. Then, as he came closer, we realized it was Peron with what we thought was a curious and profuse grin.

After such a day, it was incredible that Peron managed to keep his sense of humor. Or, that is what appeared to be the case — until he was within 20 yards of me and I understood he found nothing at all funny in what was happening! Peron was yelling: "I have no brakes!! I have no brakes!!" He desperately pulled his foot out of the pedal and started dragging it across the ground like a motocross rider, trying to stop. But it was having no effect.

Realizing that Peron really couldn't stop — and that his "smile" was really a grimace of frozen fear and panic — I stepped into the road in an attempt to catch or slow him down before he sped through the intersection. But then he steered his bike toward the rear end of one of the team cars, sparking fears among us that he was going to run right into the back of it.

At the very last moment, Peron made a daring dive for the roof rack of the car. As his bike went skidding, he wrapped his arms around one cross bar on the rack, while his body slammed into the car. Rushing to his aid, I grabbed him under the arms and pulled his bike out from under him at the same time.

"Are you all right?" I exclaimed.

All I got in response was a bunch of Italian curses, followed in English by "I had no f-ing brakes!"

He limped off to the showers as a few of our riders were coming out and, dare I say it, I couldn't help but chuckle to myself at the sight of Peron's face as he was coming down that hill. Cruel isn't it? But then, professional cycling in Europe is full of such half-funny, half-serious incidents.

When we finally got back to the team hotel, it was snowing harder than ever. George and I unloaded the bikes quickly and quietly as the light faded and the temperature dropped.

"Where's the bike stand, Scott?" asked George as he searched in the back of the team cars.

"Damn!" I exclaimed, "I forgot it, George." And we both saw a day that we both thought couldn't get any worse, just do so. Since we had only one work stand, I washed the race bikes, as George put the spare bikes and wheels away. It was too cold to wash all the spare bikes, too, so George just gave them a quick spray before stowing them.

As I washed the race bikes, I noticed that all the brake pads were completely gone … in just a few hours. A full set of brake pads can last months in good weather, but in bad conditions the grit and dirt on the road can wear them down in less than a day's racing.

With only one stand, we were forced to set up a little assembly line for working on the bikes. George pulled out all the brake pads and gave me new sets of wheels to change on each bike. In races like De Panne, a different set of wheels is automatically fitted each day, without checking the old ones — which are later inspected by the mechanic who travels straight to the next hotel instead of following the race by car.

This procedure is followed because 75 percent of the wheels won't be good enough to use the next day. The tires or rims are probably ruined, and time spent checking over each wheel in the dark and cold isn't very efficient.

More equipment is ruined in the Three Days of De Panne, Tour of Flanders and Paris-Roubaix than in any other period of racing during the year — and probably almost as much as the rest of the year combined!

I remember the first bike I worked on at that 1995 De Panne race was that of Frankie Andreu, who is one of the best riders and people I've had the opportunity of working with. The whole of his gear-shifting system didn't work. It was frozen solid! I felt a little panic begin to creep up on me at the thought of overhauling all the riders' shifting systems. Even by the time I had finished changing all of Frankie's shift cables, my hands were frozen and I could barely hold a tool. I kept changing gloves, but everything was wet and frozen. My work suit was completely soaked through, and I was shaking badly.

Every effort to fix the system had been in vain — the shifting was still poor. It was slightly better, but I realized that it was just too cold to work properly. The rest of the bikes were no better, and I had to admit to myself that perfection was not realistic in such cold conditions. The most important thing was the knowledge that the bikes were safe.

By the time I had finished the last bike, the snow had turned to freezing rain and a sheet of ice had started to form on my work suit. I was colder than I had ever been in my life, and the pain in my hands was excruciating. We closed the truck and headed for the hotel, unable to recall a time when we had ever been so grateful to finish work. The fact that I fell asleep while soaking in the bathtub, and then went to bed without having any dinner, proved that!

I have worked in some terrible conditions … far too many times. But that day was by far the worst. Days like that were ones on which I really gained respect for the riders, and their ability to overcome and suffer such conditions day after day. If anyone thinks the job of a professional bike rider is glamorous, then come to De Panne and the classics, and see for yourself!

All three of the northern classics have a separate identity. The Tour of Flanders is raced through the heart of the war-torn region of Flanders, and over most of its infamous and very steep cobbled climbs. Then, a week later, comes the granddaddy of the classics: Paris-Roubaix. One of the most intense and grueling races in cycling, Paris-Roubaix winds its way from Compiègne, 80km north of Paris, through the relatively flat French countryside and then across more than 20 sections of cobblestoned *pavé*, each of them up to four kilometers long.

The next Sunday sees a totally different type of race: Liège-Bastogne-Liège. Known as La Doyenne, because it is the oldest classic in cycling, the hilly Belgian race is rated by many as the hardest classic of all. Starting at Liège in the heart of the Ardennes — an area of steep, rolling hills and beautiful forests — it makes its way south to Bastogne and then turns around for the return to Liège.

TOUR OF FLANDERS

The Tour of Flanders, which was first held in 1913, has always been one of my favorite races to work, and is one of the most spectacular to watch. Many of the spring races in Belgium take in the infamous Flemish cobbled climbs, or bergs. But the Tour of Flanders is the only one that incorporates almost all of them. The race provides the drama and intensity of Paris-Roubaix, while also having the speed and excitement of the finale in Milan-San Remo.

For many foreigners, Belgium is a small and relatively unknown country, but the first thing any newcomer notices is that Belgians take their culture and national identity very seriously. Eddy Merckx and the Tour of Flanders are as famous in Belgium as Michael Jordan and the Super Bowl are in the U.S. And, remember, the Super Bowl has been around for only 30 years; the Tour of Flanders has been in existence for almost 90!

Locals break into a fever of excitement as the day of the race draws near. The Tour of Flanders is the only thing they want to talk about. And with Motorola's European base being in Belgium, everyone — from the mail carrier to the bank manager — wanted to know which of our riders might win.

Their enthusiasm was demonstrated when we returned to Motorola's Harelbeke headquarters after Lance Armstrong won the 1993 World Road Championship in Oslo. Our landlord covered the office entrance with flowers and a big banner saying: "Congratulations." Unfortunately, we never produced the same kind of result on our home turf of Flanders.

While these April classics were tough to ride and work, they also had their compensations. Because they took place near our H.Q., we could go home and sleep in our own beds when each race was over. When you spend so much time on the road in a year, sleeping at home quickly becomes a luxury everyone misses.

For the riders, one of the more stressful factors of Flanders and Paris-Roubaix is their physically demanding characters. It is a constant struggle to get to and stay at the front of the peloton, particularly when approaching the cobbled sectors or climbs. If there is a split, or someone crashes and blocks the entire road for too long, the race can be over for those at the back. In the wet, the cobbled climbs of Flanders are particularly treacherous. And the sight is all too common: As soon as one rider crashes on an uphill, everyone behind loses momentum, is brought to a halt, and probably ends up walking.

In the 1994 Tour of Flanders, I was in the team car with Jim Ochowicz when the race entered the final and crucial stretches of the race. When we hit a cobbled section with every team car jockeying for position, anticipating a flurry of flat tires from the riders in front, you could feel the electricity in the air. Team directors are nervous in such situations ... and who wouldn't be? As they drive at the limit, trying to maintain their place in the line, motorbikes are flying by with no room to spare, while delayed riders are working their way back to the field, riding close between the cars. To an outsider, it's pandemonium. To us, it's simply the Tour of Flanders.

In the middle of this tense phase of the race, the GB team was summoned on the radio to service one of its riders. Within seconds, the car came accelerating up from behind, its driver blasting the horn. The Italian team's stranded rider, a few cars ahead of us, was Max Sciandri, an Italian who now races for Britain, and who was with Motorola in 1992, 1993 and 1996. While European race rules stipulate that riders must be serviced on the right side of the road, Max couldn't get across the road from where he was on the left. The race was simply going too fast.

Sciandri had no choice but to pull over on the left, forcing his GB team car to skid to an abrupt halt right behind him. Team cars always stop behind the riders to protect them, as well as the attending mechanic and directeur sportif, from passing traffic.

As we sped toward the GB car and prepared to overtake it, we noticed a police motorcyclist on our left. He was also about to pass the GB car — even though there was barely enough room! Right then, the GB mechanic's door swung open and in a brief instant I saw the leg of the mechanic as he prepared to jump out and attend to Max — just before the police motorcycle crashed directly into the door at over 50 kph. Then, another cyclist right behind the motorcyclist who had nowhere to go, plowed right into the back of the motorbike, with the multiple impact bending the GB car door backward! Turning around, I saw the GB mechanic get out of the car and slowly make his way through the carnage of twisted metal and bodies. Not looking and making sure that the way was clear nearly cost him his life.

After incidents like that, it's easy to understand the reason for the "right-side" service rule. When servicing from the right, it isn't necessary to check for traffic as you are on the protected side of the road. But when you have no choice but to service on the left, you have to check before opening the car door. That GB mechanic learned the hard way.

Bike mechanics have to remember that safety is their most important priority. I've seen young and over-enthusiastic mechanics do stupid things during bike races — like changing bent handlebars after a crash while on the roof of a moving van, and prematurely jumping out of a team car before it has slowed enough. One incident from my career before I joined Motorola firmed my belief in this philosophy.

While working for the Coors Light team during the 1991 Tour DuPont — at a time when back-up support for riders wasn't as well organized in the U.S. as it is in Europe — I was asked to go in the neutral support van, as the personnel didn't have much experience. After agreeing, I realized there were no seats in the back.

I spent most of the day sitting on a spare wheel, as nothing really happened in the race. But suddenly, a hand went up from the peloton. It was Davis Phinney, a Coors Light rider and our best sprinter. He said he had broken a buckle on one of his Shimano shoes. There was 15km to go and the race seemed destined to end in a bunch sprint. He was concerned about getting his shoe ready for the finale.

I gave him a toe strap and he rode off. Then, when he started fiddling with it, he couldn't get the strap around his foot and back through the hole in the strap. He came back for me to do it. I told him to hang onto the van, which had a sliding door that was open at the time. Clocking about 55 kph, he hung on as I reached through the bike frame to fix the strap, which was on the far foot.

It was just after fixing it and telling Davis all he had to do was tighten the strap that it happened…. Davis looked down, saw the strap and let go of the van with his left hand. For a split second — before grabbing the handlebars with his left hand and reaching down to tighten the strap — he didn't have his hand on the bars at all. Simultaneously, the van moved to the center of the road and passed over a line of "cat's eyes" reflective dots so quickly that the bump took his front wheel from under him. Davis's bike went under the van as he hit the asphalt. Hearing the noise ... boom, boom, boom ... I thought he had been run over!

Davis somersaulted like a stunt man in a movie. The van stopped and I ran back. He was holding his leg. He was screaming in pain ... hollering! It seemed like he had broken his leg ... and we did it! I couldn't believe what had happened.

When he finally pulled his hands away ... there wasn't a mark on his leg. But in a matter of seconds, a huge purple welt started rising and stuck through the skin. His leg wasn't broken, but Davis was still taken by ambulance to the hospital.

As for his bike, it was unrecognizable. I had never seen a bike that had been so destroyed. Every tube was either broken, dented, bent or squashed. The only parts that weren't damaged were the head tube and seatpost. Also, the lower half of the derailleur had been ripped out. Dare I say, I still have it ... painted red and on a key chain ... a memento that reminds me how dangerous this sport can be.

PARIS-ROUBAIX

On the Wednesday after the Tour of Flanders comes the Belgian semi-classic, Ghent-Wevelgem, which has a few cobblestone sections. But in the back of everyone's minds is the race ahead: Paris-Roubaix, otherwise known as "The Hell of the North," which was first raced in 1896. And it's on the Thursday or Friday before — when the cyclists do a training ride over the last 60km or so of the Paris-Roubaix course — that we gave the riders their special bikes for the race.

For most of the riders, these are the only days when they can try out their new mounts, designed and built-up specifically to cater to the 50km of cobbles in Paris-Roubaix. Between all the races and travel beforehand, time is simply too limited to find any other occasion.

What makes a bike for Paris-Roubaix so different from the others used by our riders? First of all, the frames made to accommodate front-end suspension in the forks. Putting suspension forks on a bike that isn't designed for them raises the entire front end. And as a result, this raises the bottom bracket, making the bike more unstable and the seat angle too relaxed to position the saddle properly. It also puts the existing saddle position too far back.

The chainstays (the two tubes parallel to the chain on either side of the rear wheel) are also lengthened, making the bike more stable. Some teams still follow the traditional practice of putting in forks with more rake (more bend in the bottom) and unscrewing the dropout screws all the way in the back. This makes the bike more stable by lengthening the wheel base.

It has always been interesting to watch new riders or neo-pros when they see the cobblestones of Paris-Roubaix for the first time. They always think that since they've raced in Belgium, they've seen the worst; but nothing can prepare you for Paris-Roubaix … nothing!

Pavé is the French word for cobblestones. And these aren't just any old cobblestones. Most of these sections are centuries old and difficult to walk on, never mind riding your bike on them. The Forest of Wallers-Arenberg provides one of the worst sections, with potholes sometimes reaching two feet across. When bikes ride into holes like that, they don't make it out!

One year when the Motorola team was training there, I was waiting for the last rider to arrive near the finishing site of the Roubaix velodrome. It was pouring rain and cold, and the riders were covered in mud. I finally saw the last rider appear in the distance: Steve Swart from New Zealand. He rolled up and tossed his bike up against the car and I couldn't help but smile at the sight of him caked from head to toe in mud and dirt. Swart looked up and growled: "This isn't bike racing. This is stupid!" In a way Steve was right. Paris-Roubaix isn't really a bike race, it's a lesson in survival.

My first Paris-Roubaix with the team was in 1992 and my responsibility was to organize the support in the Wallers forest section. Normally, we had support personnel positioned throughout the forest with wheels and spare bikes because it's the worst section of cobbles in the race and the team cars are always far behind. The chances of getting a flat there are 50-50. Because the race is so fast and splits up as soon as it hits the first several sections of cobbles, the first cars can be up to five minutes behind the leaders by the time they reach Wallers.

It's amazing to see the thousands of fans who crowd the road through the forest from end to end of the 2.4km stretch. Most of the riders try to come by on a small dirt path that parallels the "road" on the right, to avoid the brutal cobblestones. But more often than not, the massing of so many spectators makes it impossible for them to pull this off.

Watching and waiting for the approaching race — while standing on my tip toes to get a better view over the crowd — I was shocked to see that the first riders were no more than 50 yards from me. Quickly grabbing my wheels and hoping to spot one of our riders, the crowd made it impossible for me to see a thing. Even had a rider passed within reach of me, he would never have recognized or heard me over the roar of the crowd. It was a hopeless exercise.

While continuing to watch for a Motorola rider, I was suddenly pulled back violently. I turned to see that the person who had grabbed me so aggressively was a spectator making the way for Jan Schur — a German rider on our team. He was making a brave bid to ride the dirt path, which I and the rest of the crowd had been standing on. Despite the odds, he was obviously determined not to let the crowd force him onto the cobbles. Screaming at the top of his lungs, his cries for a clear line were drowned by the roar of the fans. Even though the spectators were becoming slower and slower in moving out of his way, Jan was still relentless in his charge. He nearly hit one person, then brushed another. And the shocked expression on people's faces as they tried to jump out of the way mirrored their bewilderment as to where he had come from. Then, a man standing with his back to the race, came into Jan's path. Miraculously, he looked over his shoulder just in time to see the man next to him move out of Jan's way. But after he jumped across the ditch to escape a collision, Jan was on a collision course with a woman sitting in a lawn chair. She was gripping the arm rests with a look of terror as she realized it was too late to move. That sight of Jan hurtling toward her will rest with me forever. He hit the chair squarely and was launched over the handlebars as the chair crumpled under the impact, throwing the poor woman into the mud.

Already running, and hoping that I wouldn't be hit from behind by a rider or team car, I got to Jan as he was picking himself up out of the mud. I helped him onto his bike, but amid the confusion he didn't even realize or care who I was. If it hadn't have been me, it would have been a spectator. After pushing him off, I ran back to the lady and helped, along with another man, pull her from the mud. Thankfully, she was unhurt, apart from shock and wounded pride — made all the more painful by a man who was laughing like Santa Claus.

No sooner had I grabbed my wheels than Frankie Andreu passed me with a flat tire. And as he rode on hoping to get a new wheel from team helpers at the other end of the forest, as I was too late and he had not seen me anyway. I still laugh when I replay the scene in my head. The look on her face!

When the big day finally arrives, the atmosphere of a team is electric. All the work and preparation for this race has been wrapped up, and how it will pay off is in the hands of the riders.

Motorola experimented with many different types of equipment — from suspension forks and stems to double handlebar tape and rear sprocket "pie protectors," to stop the chain from going in the spokes during heavy vibration and impact. From a mechanic's standpoint, Paris-Roubaix is a fun event because we get an opportunity to be a little more creative, which is not the case in other races.

Motorola tried both suspension forks and stems and were successful with both. One advantage with the suspension stems is that they didn't require a new bike in order to be fitted properly, unlike a fork. Also, the rider was able to easily lock out the suspension when desired, such as on the regular roads in between each cobbled sector.

However, the overall performance of a suspension fork is better. Beside the feet, of course, the two main contact points between the bicycle and rider are the saddle and handlebars. A suspension stem reduces the vibration in the handlebar and its affects on the arms and upper body of the rider, but does nothing to reduce vibration in any other part of the rider through the saddle. Whereas, a suspension fork absorbs road shock and vibration before it ever enters the bike, thus greatly reducing its affects on the rider, making it much more effective at absorbing shock and vibration. Unfortunately, there is not an easily adjustable lock-out feature as there is with the stem.

It's also important to use the least amount of tire pressure possible in wet, slippery and/or muddy conditions for the best possible traction. The only problem is that as pressure is reduced, there is increased chance of a "pinch flat" (a flat that occurs when the rim hits a bump and pinches the tube, creating two small "snake bite" holes). The use of suspension forks minimizes those chances as well, allowing tire pressure to be reduced even more.

The number of spare wheels needed for an event like Paris-Roubaix is extreme. From the beginning of the season, Motorola saved all the wheels that had been dinged or damaged slightly in earlier races and weren't good enough for regular racing. For example, in 1995 we had 26 pairs of spare wheels available at numerous places along the course to save riders from waiting for the team car.

On all of these wheels, tires designed especially for Paris-Roubaix are glued on — in Motorola's case over the past few years they were Vittoria Utmost tires. About twice the diameter of normal racing tires, these require less pressure for better traction, offer more protection from pinch flats and, importantly, give a much softer ride. They are also an "all-weather" tire, something relatively new in the past few years, which handles better in poor conditions. Finally, when the race is over, all these tires are pulled off and the wheels cut down and rebuilt into new racing wheels. A few other final touches are made to bikes for Paris-Roubaix, like the use of double handlebar tape to reduce vibration from the cobbles.

In the 1994 Paris-Roubaix, I was in the team car with Jim Ochowicz. It was a brutally wet and muddy race, with the field leaving the start at Compiègne under a blanket of snow that turned to rain after 40km. After about half of the cobbled sections, we had been lucky to have only suffered one flat tire against the nine they had at the same point in 1993.

For the riders, it was a veritable struggle to stay upright on the slippery course. Everyone falls at least once in a race like Paris-Roubaix (under wet conditions), some riders as many as 10 times! But on top of the weather, what makes the day so hard for riders is the fact that the older cobbled roads are very arched. After all the years of horse-and-cart traffic, the sides of the pavé sections have sunk, leaving an extremely high center in most cases. In wet and slippery conditions like those in 1994, the only safe spot to ride is in the middle. The sides are extremely sloped and the very edges are full of water and mud.

We passed riders stricken with a variety of problems on the side and saw Dag-Otto Lauritzen, a former Motorola rider then riding with TVM, picking himself up after falling. A minute or two later, Ochowicz moved the car to the right hand side of the road, coming dangerously close to the thick deep mud off the side of the road, yet wanting to give Dag-Otto room to get through.

Jim was getting dangerously close to the edge of the road, making me a touch nervous about the thought of getting stuck in this mud!! Suddenly those fears became very real. As Dag-Otto seemingly cruised by, concentration etched across his face, the car slipped off the side of the road. Jim tried to bring the car into the middle of the road again. But the feeling of a slight jolt from behind — that of the rear wheel slipping off the side of the road into the mud — confirmed that his efforts were in vain.

Jim sensed what was happening and hit the accelerator to try and get us out. And for a brief moment it seemed like we might make it. But the front wheels were spinning on the slippery cobbles and the momentum of the rear wheel slipping off the road only carried us back into the mud with a sudden thud. We were stuck solid.

More attempts to drive out all failed, and it was inevitable that sometime soon I would have to get out and push. That moment came when I looked out the window to my right and saw mud just below the bottom of the door. Jumping out, I nearly fell as my right foot sunk almost to my knee in mud. Then, after pulling my foot out and finding firmer ground, I clambered to the back of the car to start pushing; but even that was useless. As Jim accelerated, I pushed, and the spinning wheels only came closer to being submerged.

All this was becoming a spectacle for the throng of nearby fans. Although, as happy as they were to watch our predicament, any attempt to get them to help by yelling: "*Poussez! Poussez!*" (push, push) landed on deaf ears. As I pushed from behind, they all just stood there motionless, as if transfixed by a TV screen. I couldn't believe it, thinking that any die-hard cycling fan would jump at the chance to lend a hand.

With time running out, I shelved my frustrations and ran around the left side of the car to the right front wheel, hoping that by getting to the other front wheel on the pavé, we would have a better chance of getting out.

"Gas it when I say!!" I yelled to Jim.

Then, bending over the front fender and digging my feet into the heavy mud and bracing my hands and shoulder against the fender just above the wheel, I gave the go-ahead. However, Jim had the wheel pointed hard left, and as I looked down onto the tread of the tire, I realized the critical mistake I had made. The car was front-wheel drive. Too late to do anything, I simply closed my eyes and mouth tightly, heard the engine roar and wheel spin, and stoically waited to be bombarded by flying mud.

I was covered from head to toe in a thick layer of mud, especially my face. Mud was up my nose, in my mouth, ears and eyes. I wasn't a happy camper — unlike most of the spectators who were now in hysterics. Still, I probably would have been doing the same thing if I'd been in their shoes. But then I wasn't. I was in my shoes, two feet deep in mud and really pissed!

Inspired by my bad temper, I walked up to one laughing fan, looked at him right in his face and yelled, "*Poussez!!*" while pointing to the car. Amazingly, he obliged, as did a few others. With five people, it was no problem and the car came out on the first try. Then, after giving a hearty "*merci*" we hit the rough roads of Paris-Roubaix once again.

When the race was over and I was walking back and forth between the truck and team cars to unload the equipment, my ego received a nice massage when about 20 people asked for my autograph. I couldn't figure out why until someone stopped me and asked if I were looking for the showers. Then it clicked ... I suddenly realized I looked like one of the riders. Certainly, I could have done with a shower, but the fact that Paris-Roubaix was over — for another year at least — was enough to give me the relief I needed.

LIÈGE-BASTOGNE-LIÈGE

What makes the April classics so special is that they are incredibly hard and grueling races — but for different reasons. For instance, it's very rare that riders compete in both Paris-Roubaix and Liège-Bastogne-Liège. Paris-Roubaix doesn't require any climbing skills since the course is dead flat, but it does demand a strong will to endure and overcome great amounts of pain and suffering from the endless and unmerciful cobblestones. On the other hand, Liège-Bastogne-Liège — known as La Doyenne because it's the oldest classic, dating from 1892 — not only requires great strength and power, but also finesse and climbing ability. The steep hills of the Belgian Ardennes break many a rider's spirits.

Motorola's hopes for victory in the spring of 1994 rode on Lance Armstrong, even though his early-season results had been disappointing. But that wasn't Armstrong's problem alone; the team's entire spring campaign had failed to live up to expectations. Basically, by the time Liège-Bastogne-Liège arrived in mid-April, team morale was at an all-time low.

As Liège-Bastogne-Liège neared, I found it was becoming harder to maintain a positive attitude — especially as the last big spring classic had arrived and the likelihood of a good result seemed out of reach. Making Motorola's chances even gloomier was the fact that in this race, riders can't rely on luck to win — unlike Paris-Roubaix. Only a great rider in the best shape of his life can win. There is no faking it in Liège-Bastogne-Liège.

By the halfway point of the 1994 edition, a third of the peloton had already dropped out as the endless climbs and rolling hills took their toll.

However, Lance still seemed to be riding surprisingly well with 80km to go, when the pace was high and the number of casualties grew with every kilometer.

Then, a brutal attack went off the front of the field, splintering the peloton like an axe would a log, and after a series of counterattacks a small breakaway group formed. In the car, we listened to the race radio intently, hoping that Lance had made it up there, but believing deep down that the chances were small.

"Argentin, Berzin, Furlan….," the radio blared, accounting for those riders who made the selection.

"Not again," I thought, "all of the Gewiss team."

Gewiss had dominated that spring with victory after victory. A few days after Liège-Bastogne-Liège they did it again by claiming a one-two-three finish with the same riders in the Flèche Wallonne — a very difficult classic in the same area, which is normally held a few days before Liège-Bastogne-Liège (but a few days later in 1994).

Finally, after hearing the name "Rominger," came the two words we all wanted to hear: "… and Armstrong." I couldn't believe my ears. Lance was in there! Our disappointment had suddenly been replaced with new hope.

And for all of us, it was another reminder that Lance — who only two weeks earlier couldn't do anything right — was such an extraordinary athlete. The previous year, he had won the world title. Now, here he was in a decisive break with the world's best in one of the hardest classics.

A chase group did organize itself in pursuit of the leaders — who were working well together, with four-time race winner Moreno Argentin doing most of the work. After half an hour of gaining and losing ground, the chase began to falter. And in a matter of minutes, it was all over. The break with Lance was speeding on its way to the finish at Liège.

After the team cars with riders in the break joined the leaders, I did a quick double check of my spare wheels to make sure I was ready if anything happened with Lance. Then I sat back, trying not to let Jim and Hennie Kuiper, who were both in the Motorola car, make me nervous.

After all his early work, Argentin was now just sitting at the back of the break, looking as if he were in trouble and in danger of being dropped. Mentioning this to our two directors, Hennie replied: "No way! A professional like Argentin knows his body — and this race — far too well to let that happen."

Hennie was right. Argentin at that time was one of the smartest and most experienced riders in professional cycling. He was too smart to make such an error … or so we all thought! But we watched in amazement as the race favorite was slowly dropped on the next climb and lost contact with the breakaway for good. How was this possible? Why did he work so hard when the break was first away?

After a while we began to piece together what had happened. When the break was first away, it didn't have much of a lead. After talking with his two teammates in the break (Eugeni Berzin and Georgio Furlan), he must have realized he was not the strongest. And seeing that the riders in the break were in no mood to work, Argentin probably proceeded to pull the break and hope one of his teammates won. Later, Lance said that that was one of the most difficult parts of the race. In fact, he had almost been dropped, having not fully recovered from the initial effort to make the break.

Up front, all eyes were on Rominger. He had let it be known that a victory at Liège-Bastogne-Liège was on his shopping list after finishing second to Denmark's Rolf Sørensen in 1993. When Rominger says he's going for a win, he's always hard to beat.

Entering Liège and on the approach to the finish at Ans, less than 10km out of the Ardennes capital, Armstrong was still looking good. Although everyone was looking to Rominger to make the winning move….

The anticipation in the Motorola team car was intense as the race wound its way through the streets of downtown Liège and neared Ans. It was just after the route took a hard left to start the final climb, at the 5km-to-go mark, that our concentration was awoken by the race radio blaring out: "Mapei! Mapei!" I instinctively jumped, fearing the radio announcer said Motorola. Thankfully he didn't….

Glancing out the window to see what happened, I saw Rominger slowly losing contact with the break, with his hand raised in the air. He obviously had a problem. Looking down at his bike as we drove past him, I saw his back wheel had broken a spoke and was wobbling all over the place.

It was typical of Rominger. He always pushes the limits of dependability with his equipment and ends up having technical problems. He broke an ultralight carbon-fiber seatpost in Milan-San Remo a few weeks earlier, and was forced to change bikes a few times at critical points in the race.

Here, with the race speeding up, it soon became clear that Rominger would not make it back in time; his wheel change cost him too many precious seconds. Meanwhile, our chances for victory had increased dramatically. Of the now four leaders, the favorite was Furlan, who had won Milan-San Remo and was in the best form of his career.

Passing the 4km-to-go mark, even the butterflies in my stomach were fluttering like crazed bees. Our team had never been this close to a World Cup victory. Then the race radio alerted us to an attack. We all strained to see who it was. And after wondering if the blue jersey was Furlan's, we saw it was that of his Russian teammate, Berzin. He didn't appear to be far up the road, so we watched with anticipation to see who would chase. However, with his teammate Furlan ready to cover any chases, Berzin seemed to have squashed any winning hopes we had for Lance. As his lead increased, he looked over his shoulder to the others hesitating. Sensing the opportunity to broaden his lead further, Berzin turned on the gas and sprinted out of the saddle to distance his former companions for good. He took 300 meters in what seemed like seconds, proving that his initial attack had not even been 100 percent!

Unfortunately for us, Berzin stayed away to the finish to win, while Lance was left to take the sprint for second place. It was a dramatic and memorable finale, one I will always remember. Why? Basically, it marked the turning point of our season. While there was still the Amstel Gold Race in one week's time, Lance's rediscovery of form gave the team renewed hope — especially for the upcoming and all-important trip to the U.S. and the Tour DuPont.

chapter four

Positioning
and Frame
Geometry

Y ou probably already know that picking a frame based on, say, its love-
ly paint job is not what one would call a good strategy. Design,
materials and construction all play an important role, but even the
most methodically constructed frame, made of the best materials in the world
won't do you much good if you aren't comfortable on it. And while comfort is critical, you also have to be certain that you end up in an efficient
position that allows you to generate the most power.

One might think that finding a good position on the bike would not be
all that difficult. But it is. Even some of the world's top professionals ride
with poor positions. Take the case of Frenchman Luc Leblanc, who won
the 1994 World Road Championship at Agrigento, Italy. The following
spring, I remember watching him and noting that his saddle was so high
that my knees began to ache just looking at him. It was unbelievable that
something so obviously wrong could go unchanged for so long. It can
take riders many years to find the perfect bike position and, because it
can become an ever-evolving process, most of my recommendations are
merely good starting points.

Clearly, what drives any vehicle is its engine. In the case of a bicycle

you, and in particular your legs are the engine. So, let's start by examining
the critical relationship between the rider's hips, legs and feet.

The position of the foot in relation to the pedal spindle is very important. Some riders prefer to have their feet slightly forward or backward
from the spindle, but the best place to start and the most appropriate is to
place the ball of the foot directly over it.

Some riders believe that by moving the cleat a bit forward, keeping
more of the foot behind the spindle, they can get added leverage and
power. This approach, however, puts a lot of stress on the Achilles ten-
don and strains the calf muscle, something that may not suit all riders.
For Greg LeMond it didn't seem to be a problem. He relied on a lot of
"ankling" in his pedal stroke and, therefore, preferred to have his cleat
positioned further forward. Others riders, like Davis Phinney, had no
ankling and their feet stayed at an almost constant angle throughout the entire
stroke. In Phinney's case, his toes almost always pointed slightly down.

There is one sure way to make certain that the ball of your foot is properly placed over the pedal spindle. First, drill a small hole in the bottom of
your shoe as close to the ball of your foot as you can guess. (You'll probably
want to do this with your shoe off.) Then, put your shoe on without a sock
and, with a marking pen, make a dot on your bare foot through the hole
you just drilled. Take your shoe off and measure the distance from the
dot you marked to the ball of your foot. Use that measurement to find where
the ball of your foot would rest in relation to the sole of the shoe. With the
ball of your foot marked on the sole, make a mark on the edge of the
sole in line with the ball of your foot mark. Now, make sure that lines
up directly above the pedal spindle while your shoe is flat (or in your natural pedaling position) and your crank is in the 3 o'clock position.

Your toe-in and toe-out adjustment is also very important, and any
changes made in this adjustment should be made gradually. The best
place to start is in the neutral position with your feet slightly toed out.
Depending on your walking style and the natural toe-in or out of your feet,
this adjustment will vary from person to person. Most riders have a slight-

ly toed-out position.

It is also important to make sure that the foot offset (the distance from your foot to the center of the bicycle) is the very nearly the same for both feet. With your shoe clipped into the pedal, you can check the offset, measuring the distance from the edge of the sole of your shoe to the seat tube. The measurements for both shoes should be within a millimeter or two. It is also important that your feet be properly spaced from one another. For years, Lance Armstrong had problems with his feet hurting, as well as a chronically sore back. Both were beginning to affect his performance until a friend recommended that he widen his stance on the bike by just a couple of millimeters. So we put a couple of washers on the insides of his pedal spindles and — *Voilà!* — there was an almost immediate improvement.

Lance could not believe how much better he felt after such a seemingly minor adjustment. From then on, Lance never got on a bike without washers between the pedal spindles and crank arms. His problem before had been that his feet were spaced too narrowly, and that resulted in his placing a great deal of pressure on the outside of each foot. The resulting pain caused him to compensate by changing his natural pedaling style or shifting his position on the bike. That led to back pain and endless discomfort.

Though saddle height is an important factor in rider position and performance, it is the most common measuring error made when setting up a bike. It is also one area where everyone seems to have an opinion. Still, I think the best approach, and the one most widely accepted in the cycling world, is the rule that there should about a 25- to 30-degree bend in the leg, or your leg should form an angle of 150-155 degrees. This is the best place to start and is suitable for most riders. It is also one of the measurements that should vary the least from rider to rider, irrelevant of the type of riding they do or their physical characteristics.

When a saddle position is too low, it can be difficult to generate adequate power. Too low of a position can also stress the knees. On the other hand, a saddle too high can place even greater stress on the knees and risk injury. Sean Yates always preferred to keep the saddle of his time trial bike quite a bit higher than that of his regular road bike because he felt he could generate more power in that position. Still, he realized that the position would be too hard on his legs for everyday racing on his regular road bike.

Fore-and-aft position varies quite a bit from rider to rider. It is, of course, very dependent on an individual's physical characteristics and riding style, but a racer may find the need to adjust fore and aft depending also on the type of event they might be doing. The best fore-and-aft starting point can be determined by a simple procedure. Use a wind trainer to warm up and get comfortable on the bike. Place the cranks in a position parallel to the ground. We will be measuring the forward leg. Find the soft tissue on the front of the knee just below the knee cap, drop a plumb bob from there and see where it hangs relative to the pedal spindle. It should bisect it, or line up with it vertically. Typically, a more rearward position is preferred by power-oriented riders like Lance Armstrong and Phil Anderson. Such a position allows the rider to sit back and use a slightly larger gear. On the other hand, spinners, like Andy Hampsten for example, usually preferred a position farther forward. Almost always, whenever a young American rider joined the Motorola team and came to Europe, he invariably ended up moving his seat back slightly, and, in some cases, quite a bit.

The style and type of racing or riding also has a lot to do with this position. A more forward position is more appropriate for short, fast events where the racer is usually turning the pedals at a high cadence. Examples of this type of racing are criteriums, the most common racing in the USA; and track racing. A more rearward position tends to be suitable for longer events, like the road racing in Europe.

Although not as critical as lower-body position, upper-body positioning is an important element to the fit equation. A properly positioned upper body is important when it comes to comfort and aerodynamics.

Really, the reason we have avoided a detailed discussion of sizing frames is because your ideal position must be established before you can start sizing yourself for a new bike. This may seem hard to believe, but when determining frame size (seat tube length), seat height has almost noth-

Beth Schneider

Beth Schneider

Graham Watson

Graham Watson

Top Motorola's Alvaro Mejia raced with winner Miguel Indurain on the Galibier pass at the '93 Tour **Above** Author Scott Parr preparing a bike for Paris-Roubaix **Bottom left** Sean Yates gets a replacement bike during Paris-Nice **Left center** Phil Anderson is handed a musette by soigneur John Hendershot at the 1992 Tour DuPont

Far left Andrea Peron blew it bigtime on the Mende stage of the '95 Tour **Left** Lance Armstrong charges to another stage win at the '93 Tour DuPont **Below** Soigneur Freddie Viane greets Frankie Andreu after a Tour stage in '95 **Bottom right** Another hotel stop for Parr at the 1994 Giro d'Italia **Left center** wheels galore **Far left bottom** Parr's patented bike height and position calibrator

Beth Schneider photos

Top left Celebration time at the Tour DuPont for the Motorola team **Top right** Motorola Directeur Sportif Hennie Kuiper **Far right top** Motorola's chief mechanic George Noyes **Far right center** Working next to one of the team's Volvo trucks **Far right bottom** A big push for Mapei's Wilfried Peters after a Tour wheel change **Right** Running repairs during a spring classic **Above** Julian DeVries (right) worked with Parr at the '91 world's

Left A week before his tragic death, Fabio Casartelli (right) climbed in the Alps with teammate Stephen Swart **Above** Casartelli's death was commemorated by Lance Armstrong with his '95 Tour stage win at Limoges **Right top** Catching up with the news at the Tour "village" **Far right** Team Doctor Massimo Testa **Lower right** Armstrong with the boss Jim Ochowicz **Right center** Wheel changes are the same the world over

Beth Schneider photos

Top Yates goes for it at the '93 Tour prologue **Right** A wheel for Max Sciandri from Mechanic Geoff Brown **Above** A rare moment of peace for Parr before a '94 Tour stage in the Alps.

ing to do with it. When determining frame size, remember that the smallest frame possible is the most ideal because it is lighter and will typically handle better because of its smaller size. "Drop" needs to be considered when
determining seat-tube length. The drop is the vertical distance between the
top of the saddle and the top of the handlebars or how much lower the stem
is than the saddle. A rider with more flexibility will have a lower front
end than a rider with less flexibility. Ideally the lower you can go and still
be comfortable, the better. Also to be taken into account is the head-tube
length. The top tube that connects the two is always flat, and the head-tube
length should be determined by the drop or stem height. For example, two
different riders both riding a 58cm bike when only taking their leg lengths
into account, may in fact have very different "ideal" frame sizes when
taking into account the "drop" factor.

If your stem is as low as it can go and you feel comfortable, then you probably can afford to go down in frame size. Now that extra long seatposts are
readily available, the rider's inseam measurement has become much less
important and drop much more so when determining the optimum seat-
tube length or frame size. Drop generally increases as the size of the rider
increases, because larger riders have longer arms, enabling them to reach a
lower handlebar position. That is why you typically see much more seatpost sticking out of a 60cm bike than you would out of a 53cm. A small
rider on a 53cm frame with average flexibility may have a drop of only 6cm
while a large rider on a 60cm may have a drop of 12cm.

Unfortunately, one minor snag in this whole formula is that unless you
are buying a custom bike built specifically for you, your options may be limited. When deciding what your ideal frame size is, it is important to consider the role of top-tube length. In an "off-the-rack" stock frame, seat- and
top-tube lengths are directly related. Even if it is possible for you to drop
down in seat-tube size, you may be hindered from doing this because
your top-tube length will generally shorten as well. If you are already running a long stem, this may not be ideal. Because of that, most professional teams have custom bikes built for their riders, because stock bikes may

not be the ideal for them. However, there are still some teams that use stock bikes because making customs would cost a fortune. The Saturn team, for example, equipped each of its racers with stock Trek OCLV frames. The cost of customs in this case would be prohibitive.

The Italian manufacturers typically make bikes with shorter top tubes because the Italians and Spanish generally have shorter upper bodies than people in the U.S. So, when deciding what bike to buy, don't just get a Colnago because you've always wanted a Colnago. Get a bike that fits you well. Look to see what manufacturers offer a wide variety of sizes. For instance, Ben Serotta in the United States stocks a wide range of sizes because he believes proper sizing is very important and realizes that there are lots of riders with different shapes and sizes out there.

Finally, the last measurement to consider is "reach" — the combination of top tube and stem length. Ultimately, you want to have an upper-body position that is as low as possible while maintaining comfort, and long enough that your back is somewhat flat (not hunched). You also need to be comfortable on the drops and hoods while maintaining a slight bend in the elbow in both positions. It's also important to have a proper-size stem relative to the size of the bike.

Weight distribution is very important, and ideally you want to have your hands over the front hub of the bike for proper bike handling. For example, you should not have a 11cm stem on a 60cm bike, nor should you consider a 14cm stem for a 52cm bike. A frame smaller than 53cm should generally be equipped with a 12cm stem or less. Bikes between 54cm and 57cm bikes should probably use a 11.5cm to 12.5cm stem, and bikes 58cm or larger should rely on stems longer than 12cm.

There is also a wide range of handlebars available, the two most common being deep- and shallow-drop bars. Most people tend to favor deep-drop bars out of habit. I think that is a mistake, unless you are a tall rider with long arms. For small- and medium-sized people, deep-drop bars make it difficult, if not impossible, to find a good position in the drops and on the brake hoods. With deep-drop bars, if the hoods are in a good position then the drops tend to be too low; and if the drops are in a good position then the hoods are too high and force you to ride predominantly in one position — which defeats the whole purpose of the bars. When I first joined the Coors Light team, there was a small rider on the team who had 44cm deep-drop bars on his bike. It was a funny sight. Whenever he rode, all you could see were these handlebars coming your way. It was like seeing a three-year-old behind the wheel of a big old Lincoln Continental.

Handlebars also come in a variety of widths — 40cm, 42cm and 44cm are the most common. Proper bar width depends on the size of the rider. A general rule of thumb is to say that 40cm bars are suitable for small riders, 42cm for medium riders, and 44cm for large riders. Of course, it also important to remember that different manufacturers measure bar width differently. For example, a 42cm Cinelli is roughly equal to a 44cm ITM.

As already stated, not all the these recommendations on positioning are ideal for everyone, and each rider's requirements will very slightly depending on their own physical characteristics. These recommendations are merely a good starting point for most people, and help them find their position or give them a standard with which to compare their current position. Furthermore, any changes should be done in slow and small increments over time, not in one fell swoop.

Generally, riders' positions evolve over time and it's important not to develop any bad habits early on, as they can be difficult to break. Most riders — even professionals — have no idea why their bike is set up the way it is, except for the fact that maybe it feels good. Part of that problem is that some changes may be made to correct other problems. Whenever there is pain or discomfort, the body tries to correct it, and this can lead to other problems. To develop a good overall position, you must calculate your position correctly from the very first step. Many people get used to the discomforts or pain from cycling because in any aerobic sport a certain amount of suffering is to be expected. That is why it can be so difficult to determine whether the discomfort you feel is from the incorrect positioning or not.

I recall one Motorola rider who constantly complained that he could not get comfortable on his time-trial bike, particularly for the team time trial. The mechanics worked and worked on his bike, changing everything possible: frames, bars, stems, saddles and position. But it was all to no avail. Finally, we realized that it was the rider. In essence, how can you be comfortable when you are pushing your body to its very limits of pain and suffering? The team time trial is *never* comfortable!

When riders are doing well, the bike is always perfect, but when they are not, many try and find a reason. Quite often it can be due to a fault with the bike, but certainly not always. In my own experience, the propensity of riders to blame their bike depended a lot on the rider. Guys like Sean Yates and Lance Armstrong never tried to find an excuse for a poor performance — whether it was the bike or something else. They were strong enough in their own minds to know that it was their responsibility alone. Unfortunately, most people — cyclists included — do not have this quality, which is a sign of a real champion. Once, a rider returned to the hotel after a race on the verge of tears, mumbling that there was something wrong with his bike. He had no idea what it was, just that he felt bad on it. It was kind of sad.

There is not any formula that will give you the perfect bike position. Position and fit rely heavily on a rider's physical characteristics and the type of cycling he or she expects to be doing. Do you have a lot of flexibility like Max Sciandri, or the tighter muscle composition of someone like Lance Armstrong? Do you like to push a big gear like Phil Anderson, or spin like Andy Hampsten? There are many answers, just as there are numerous successful racers endowed with varying qualities and physical characteristics.

Beware of the person who says he might have a universal system to determine perfect position and bike size. Nothing is perfect in life and that is doubly true in cycling.

chapter five

Homeward Bound:

Where's the Picnic?

'A change is as good as a rest," explained Sean Yates to the fan who had just asked him why he liked coming back to the United States to race. Yates and I were sitting in the Radisson Hotel restaurant, having lunch the day before the first stage of the 1995 Tour DuPont in Wilmington, Delaware.

Twelve days later, I reflected on Yates's words on the way to the airport, for my flight back to Europe, the day after Lance Armstrong clinched the race's overall victory for the first time. I couldn't remember ever being so tired. Normally I would have stopped to take a quick nap, but I didn't have enough time. Yates's words seemed inappropriate. I doubted Yates felt "rested" after this race … at least I didn't.

I had to leave the team car I was driving in the airport parking lot, for someone else to pick up. Yet, despite my fatigue, I was still very nervous about executing the mission of unloading the five bike bags, my suitcase and tool box, and getting it all into the airport and checked in while not getting the team car towed. Atlanta's airport had really boosted its security because of the upcoming Olympic Games, so there seemed little chance of being able to leave my car unattended for even a second. How I was going to get everything checked in — and I couldn't exactly leave $20,000 worth of bicycles (including Lance's race bikes for the Tour de France) on the curb while I parked the car a mile away — was as big a problem as I've ever encountered!

Pulling up to the curb at the terminal, I jumped out and immediately hailed a porter to load everything, when I noticed the security guards giving me a suspicious "once-over." I would have to take my chances. As I went through the doors and hit the refreshing air conditioning, I let out a groan upon seeing the long line to the ticket counter. After what seemed like forever, I finally made it to the front of the line, still thinking I had never been so tired in my whole life. All I wanted to do was get on that plane and sleep.

"Sir, sir!" said the airline check-in representative, awakening me from my trance at the ticket counter. "Here's your ticket. Your gate is G24. Have a nice flight." I stumbled off to the gate and breathed my first sigh of relief. It was the first time in two weeks that I didn't have anything to worry about. It was a nice feeling to look down at my watch, see there were still 35 minutes before take-off and decide there was enough time for a stress-killing beer.

Pulling up a bar stool after ordering a Sam Adams, I took the first cold sip, smiled, and secretly congratulated myself on a job well done. My mission was accomplished and the first waves of relaxation rolled easily over me. But then my stomach clenched, my eyes bolted forward and a pure jolt of panic shot through my body as I realized I had completely forgotten about the car!

Jumping up, grabbing my bag and breaking into a full sprint, I glanced down at my watch: 18 minutes before departure and counting. Running all the way through the terminal seemed like eternity, and my carry-on bag seemed to weigh 200 pounds. Whether the car had been towed or not was anyone's guess. If it were gone, there was no alternative but to get on the plane and call someone from the hotel and ask them to pick it up. And even if it were there, I still had to park it and risk missing my flight.

Approaching the glass doors, I couldn't see the car ... and the knot in my stomach grew tighter. Yet, after sprinting through the doors, the car was still sitting where I had left it — much to my surprise. I fumbled with the keys, finally got the right one in the door and hopped in. "Fourteen minutes to go." Continuing to swear at myself for forgetting about the car, wheels squealing, I accelerated away from the curb and down the ramp toward "long-term parking."

Leaving the car in the closest spot, I noticed a shuttle bus waiting. If ever I needed a break, it was then. I still had 10 minutes up my sleeve.

Jumping on the bus, I told the driver my flight was leaving in five minutes, hoping he would be sympathetic.

"I'm sorry sir, I gotta wait here four more minutes and your airline is my last stop," he replied, prompting me to reach into my pocket and pull out a $20 bill. "This is yours if we leave now and you go straight to my airline," was my reply, answered almost immediately by him flooring it so hard I lost my balance and almost fell.

"I'll get you there!" he exclaimed, tearing up the road and leaving me to wonder how I ever thought riding in a team car was dangerous....

Giving him a quick thanks as he approached my stop, my mental countdown to departure read: "Four minutes." When he was close to stopping, I was already out the door and running, hoping my watch was fast or that the flight had been delayed.

When I got to the gate, barely able to catch my breath, no one was in sight. No one. No passengers. No flight attendants. Nobody. I ran up to the gate door and peered through the glass. The plane was still there, but about to pull away. I rapped on the door, but to no avail. I had missed it....

In desperation, you can do funny things. And I was desperate. Grabbing the door knob, I expected it to be locked — especially as it was a security door only activated by a five-digit combination lock. But as I pulled on it, it swung open. It hadn't closed all the way! Were it not for all the other strife, the day would now have been remembered for being my lucky day!

After sprinting down the jetway, I saw the plane door was closed; but that didn't stop me from peering in the little window and giving a hard knock. A stewardess appeared, giving me a look that read: "What are you doing out there?" A smile was the best I could respond with, praying she would open the door. Fate proved to be on my side. She did.

"What are you doing out there?" she asked, a little perturbed that I had disrupted things.

"I'm late and the door up there was open so I just walked down," I explained, completely out of breath and soaked from head to toe in sweat. Still, I was a happy camper, despite the sea of dirty looks passengers gave me as I walked back to my seat.

"I made it!"

Now it's time for that beer!

By the time the Tour DuPont rolled around in early May, the classics had come and gone — along with my patience of working in cold, rainy and sometimes snowy conditions. So thoughts of heading home to the sunshine and warmth of the East Coast were happy ones. The Tour DuPont was the one race I always looked forward to the most and considered my favorite, but in reality it could be the biggest pain in the ass, as well.

Racing in the U.S. is quite different — the atmosphere, excitement, and overall enthusiasm for the race — from racing in Europe. I'll never forget sitting in the lobby of our hotel the night before the race started in Wilmington, Delaware. While I was talking with Steve Bauer, the race marshals meeting suddenly ended. There were hundreds of them, filing past us and out the front door for what seemed like a half-hour. They were all young people, laughing and yelling, excited about being part of the race and wearing their new Tour DuPont T-shirts. It seemed like prom had just ended.

We were getting excited about the race, just sitting there watching them go by. In contrast, the races in Europe are less colorful. There are no marshals, just police motorcyclists keeping traffic at bay and the same old officials. In Europe, it's "business as usual." At the Tour DuPont, there was almost a party atmosphere, and the enthusiasm was contagious.

Everyone who participates in the Tour DuPont enjoys it ... particularly the European team personnel and riders. They welcomed the nice change of pace. For some, it was the only time in their lives when they would see the U.S. For American staff on the Motorola team, it was always nice to be home again. While working and living in Europe was more enjoyable than any other experience in my life, I was always ready to come back to the U.S. Not having to worry about a language barrier is a pretty nice feeling. It was especially so after struggling in almost every situation with limited Spanish, Italian, French, Dutch and German.

John Hendershot, Motorola's head soigneur, once said that if you can't get it in the U.S., you don't need it. It was an amusing thought, but very true. It was always a little overwhelming to return home and go to a shopping mall that sells everything from car tires to frozen pizza, and has a full-service bank. But it was especially handy for soigneurs to have access to 24-hour grocery superstores for buying race food, and knowing they could buy ice anywhere or get it in the hotel — as opposed to having to carry a freezer in the truck. It gives everyone on a pro team peace of mind ... and some extra time.

For the Motorola team, being the big kids on the block was always nice. Whether it was getting a good spot for parking the truck, getting an extra room at the hotel or whatever, we almost always got what we wanted. Being the No. 1 team in a race was a boost, too. It was great for the ego to get all the attention and respect that we so rarely got in Europe. In Europe, we were just like everybody else; in the U.S., we were the big stars.

Despite all the positives, there were also lots of negatives. These would start in the big hotels — where the service is supposedly so great and the customer always right. I found that Americans had relatively little ability to compromise, adapt to new situations or solve a problem. We would have a far better chance of getting what we wanted in Italy, with five words of broken Italian, than in American, where cycling receives little respect ... such as in the following incident.

I had just driven non-stop with a car full of bikes from our team headquarters in Wisconsin to Atlanta for the First Union Grand Prix, a big one-day race that took place a few days before the Tour DuPont. (The all-in-a-day drive was due to fears of leaving the bikes in the car overnight.) Arriving very late that night at the Atlanta hotel — a very big and expensive one, never a good sign for visiting bike mechanics who need space to work in — I walked into reception after the doorman hassled me for leaving my car by the entrance.

"My name is Scott Parr, I'm with the Motorola cycling team for the race this weekend. Could you please tell me where the bike room is?" I asked the receptionist.

"Bike room?" he replied in a tone that indicated this was not going to be a simple chat.

"Yes, the room where all the teams are storing their bikes for the race," was my rapid-fire volley, which he returned just as smartly: "I'm sorry, we don't have anywhere for you to store your bikes."

Prepared for a long rally of verbal shots, I continued, " Well, I've got seven bikes in my car that I need to put somewhere. Is there a storage room I could put them in until we get things straightened out in the morning?"

"No, I'm afraid not," he said, proving he knew exactly what we wanted. Naïvely, I still believed that as most teams weren't arriving until the next day, perhaps the hotel hadn't yet prepared a bike room and that this receptionist was unaware of what to expect. Not to be beaten, I asked where my room was and told him I would take the bikes up to my room then for the night — even though this was not exactly what I wanted to do.

"I'm sorry, sir, that's not possible," he said, proving my theory that the U.S. is "the land of no."

"You can't tell me where my room is, why not?"

"No, not that. I mean its not possible to keep your bikes in your room; we had a problem here last year with that."

"What?" I yelled, having now lost my self-control. "What kind of problem? You mean to tell me that you had teams staying here last year and you didn't think to have a place for them to keep their bikes this year?!"

"Some of the walls in the rooms were scuffed from leaning the bikes against them."

"Can I speak to the manager?"

"He'll be in at 9 a.m., sir."

"Is there anyone else here that I can talk to?"

"No, sir, I'm the only one on duty until 5 a.m."

This is the type of situation that really gets on my nerves, and one that is typical of the U.S. racing scene. But I was not beaten, yet.

"Well what do you suggest I do then?" I said, reentering the fray of verbal battle.

"I don't know sir," he replied coldly, as if to put a cap on the entire argument.

At the end of my tether, I simply said to him that I would be taking the bikes up to my room … unless he had an alternative idea. I wondered if he would be stupid enough to try and stop me. Fortunately, he didn't, and I spent the next half-hour taking all the equipment from the team car up to my room, knowing I had to drag it all down again the next morning. Yet, while I won the battle, I knew this would not be his last stand against the horde of bike mechanics expected to arrive the next day.

It's typical at U.S. races not to have anywhere to store the bikes, a place where water is available to work on the bikes, or even a parking lot for the team vehicles. The heart of the problem is that so few people know about competitive cycling in the U.S. that hotels, cities and even police forces have no idea of the sport's unique demands.

It's a completely opposite scenario in Europe. When teams arrive at a race or hotel there is a 99.9-percent chance that a bike race has been to their village before. As a result, they know what to expect. Furthermore, most of the hotels European teams stay in are ones they've stayed at before. Quite often when Motorola arrived at a European hotel, parking was reserved for our trucks and cars, and electricity and water was already hooked up for each team to use. There was a completely different attitude in the U.S., where hotel staffs looked upon us as an inconvenience or a disruption to their everyday routines.

One year at the Tour DuPont, an Italian mechanic almost got hauled off to jail by the Virginia state troopers. In bike racing, when nature calls, riders pull over to the side of the road to relieve themselves — quite often in big groups; that's just part of bike racing. This can seem a little offensive to spectators, especially Americans, who may have never seen a bike race. However, in a six- or seven-hour race, not only do the riders need to make a pit stop, but so does everyone in the race caravan — including the team directors and mechanics. Most of the time, we try to find a relatively secluded area where there are no spectators and just pull over onto the side of the road. There isn't time to stop at a restaurant, or anything like that, as you would lose too much time.

The Virginia State troopers, thinking this was a little vulgar and inappropriate, warned everyone that if they were caught doing this in sight of the road they would be arrested. Most teams thought this was pretty amusing (Europeans are a little less inhibited when it comes to things like this), and thought that the American police were just joking. So the next day everyone forgot about it and worked the race as usual.

After two warnings from the state troopers over their loudspeaker, an Italian team car pulled over and took care of "business." The troopers pulled over behind them, and, to the horror of the Italian mechanic, handcuffed him before he even had time to do up his pants and threw him into the back of their squad car. The team director was ranting and raving in Italian trying to get them to let his mechanic go … but to no avail.

We pulled over behind the police and I jumped out and explained to them that the Italians didn't speak English, probably hadn't understood the troopers' repeated warnings and that in Europe this type of thing is normal. However, the trooper couldn't believe that such behavior was accepted anywhere.

"We don't tolerate that type of behavior in Virginia!" he yelled in his heavy Southern drawl.

After some serious diplomatic maneuvering — and, later, the gift of a jersey — the trooper released the mechanic. I was a big hero for that one; I never heard "*Grazie!*" so many times in my life, and later on whenever I was at a race and needed something, they were the first team I hit up … *no problemo!*

A few days later, the team director of that team and his team car were nowhere to be found. Not until a day later did he turn up. The Italian team director had been pulled over and arrested for speeding at 85 mph in a 45-mph zone and spent a night in jail. The morning he was missing, the staff from his team scrambled around in a panic as they had only one team car to take their riders to the start of the stage. Even though they left with a pretty poor impression of the U.S., the incident caused quite a bit of amusement in the race entourage.

Another thing that made the Tour DuPont difficult for us was the pressure. All eyes were on Motorola. And as the team had more to lose than any other, and being the biggest American team, we were always expected to dominate the race and win. In Europe though, Motorola was in a unique situation in that the team was never "at home," and so never had the pressure to win like the European teams did. Hence, when we arrived back in the U.S., our riders weren't accustomed to dealing with that kind of pressure.

But the pressure was good for the American riders. Everyone knows that a team plays better on its home field than on the road, and it's the same in cycling. French riders are better in France, Italian riders are better in Italy, and American riders are better in America.

What made it difficult for the mechanics is that during the first two-thirds of the race, every rider really went for it. In a normal stage race, a team has a designated leader or leaders and designated domestiques. Domestiques know their role and usually realize it's not their place to be really going for it, particularly in the time trials, in which they should focus on saving their energies to help their leaders later in the race.

That was never the case at the Tour DuPont. For the American riders, it was time to show their stuff, whether they were domestiques or not. Who wants to be shown up by a less-experienced American amateur racer, especially when you are a pro with the big Motorola team? For some, it was really their only chance at success, since the competition wasn't as tough and a lot of the European riders regarded the race as an American holiday.

I'm not saying that we didn't give 100-percent effort to prepare every rider's bike all the time, but there are limits on time, energy and particularly equipment. In a perfect world, maybe, you could give everyone brand new tires, or handlebar tape or bikes every day; but that's just not realistic. At the first time trial of the Tour DuPont, every rider wanted the best result possible and as a result, a different gear ratio, bike, wheels and tires. It could be a very demanding and stressful situation.

An example was the Roanoke time trial in the 1995 DuPont — which was probably the single most difficult stage I've worked on at any race that I've experienced, including the team time trial of the Tour de France. It was a very technical course, with flat sections, two long, steep climbs and dangerous descents. We were using four different kinds of wheels: disc wheels, Specialized tri-spoke wheels, deep-dish Ambrosio Alu-splinter wheels, and normal radially bladed road wheels, plus 26-inch front wheels for the time trial bikes. Then we used three types of tires: regular road tires for all conditions, dry low-profile tires for dry conditions, and wet-weather tires for bad conditions. Each rider had an option of at least two bikes: a time trial bike or a road bike with aero' bars, and some riders like Lance had as many as four options. Because of the nature of the course, it was very important to make the right equipment choices.

With the steep climbs and technical descents, it was necessary to have the comfort and familiarity of a road bike and normal wheels because disc or tri-spoke wheels are heavier and more rigid, and don't handle as well on rough descents. However, with the long flat sections, it was important to have the aerodynamic benefit of a time trial bike and aero' wheels.

If we had fulfilled every rider's demands — seven race bikes and eight or nine spare bikes all with different gear ratios; all the different combinations of wheels on hand, all the different varieties of tires for each bike prepared for all types of conditions, and ready to meet any request; plus spare wheels — a total of 224 pairs of wheels would have been needed. That's 448 wheels for one day, not including the normal road wheels for the road stages. This is pretty ridiculous, not to mention impossible. To anyone who says every rider should be treated the same, I say you do the best you can with what you have ... and keep your fingers crossed.

The prologue of the 1992 Tour DuPont typified the importance of correct equipment choice. The course followed a short, steep, cobbled climb and then, after a loop, it returned and descended on the same cobblestones. The course always made me nervous because of the great likelihood of puncturing, especially when using disc and four-spoke wheels.

These wheels are more prone to flatting because they are so rigid, and tend not to "give" like a normal rim would under impact. If you hit a pothole, for example, with a normal wheel, the rim may dent or get a flat spot before the tire bottoms out on it and creates a "pinch" flat. A disc or carbon-fiber wheel is more rigid and less prone to denting, therefore it can pinch the tire before the wheel gives. Box-shaped rims are less prone to pinch flats and more prone to denting than V-cross-sectioned rims because V-rims are more rigid.

I always felt that normal road wheels were the best choice for that course, but I knew that view would never correspond with the feeling of bike riders who wanted to use the latest equipment we could get. The best I could do was put normal road tires on all the time trial wheels, instead of the low-profile ones, which are more prone to pinch flats, and then switch them back again after the prologue. A lot of work for just 6.2 miles!

While following Phil Anderson that day, we came hurtling around the corner before the cobblestones, and I immediately saw there was something wrong — his bike appeared to be going sideways. It looked like Phil had flatted: He was having a hard time keeping his bike upright and slowing down. I immediately grabbed my wheels and then realized it was better to give him a bike, as we were only a mile or so from the finish. It seemed like forever before he stopped, while I stood in the van's doorway, waiting to jump at the perfect time.

Leaping from the door, hoping I wouldn't twist my ankle on a cobblestone, I ran around to the back of the van to get Phil's spare bike (it wouldn't fit on the normal passenger side because of the minivan's sliding door). Then, as I unclipped the bike and pulled it down, it seemed like everything was going in slow motion and that I was taking forever! After giving him his bike, pushing him off and returning to pick up his old bike, I noticed that the rear four-spoke wheel was completely destroyed. He had punctured and when the tire went flat in probably a hundredth of a second, the wheel exploded from the impact of the cobblestones on the bare rim at such a high speed. All that was left was the metal hub with pieces of carbon fiber dangling off it. How he had managed not to crash on a fast cobbled descent with no back wheel is still a mystery to me.

Phil only lost about 30 seconds with the puncture that day, which seemed unfortunate but not a real big deal at the time as Phil wasn't a favorite for the overall victory. But that year he had very good form and ended up winning three stages, and finishing fifth overall, only 60 seconds behind Greg LeMond in the final results. Had he not flatted that day, he might well have challenged LeMond for the overall title. We'll never know. That the tables can turn so quickly with a little bit of bad luck makes the sport all the more exciting.

However, the point made most clear to me from that episode was that carbon-fiber wheels were not the ideal choice for that particular course; normal road wheels would have been more appropriate. However, since cycling is, in a sense, just a big show — as well as a demanding sport — there was no way any rider would have considered not using the coolest high-tech equipment possible. Much of the sport is fueled by mind games. If a rider thinks he has a light, fast bike he'll be more motivated, and if he sees that everyone else around him has something better, he is psychologically defeated.

Another aspect that made coming to the U.S. so difficult was that most of the equipment and supplies came from Europe. For the Tour DuPont, all the European teams had their equipment sent over on a charter flight with the team and delivered to their hotels free of charge, but because we were an "American" team, we had to cover the cost of transporting equipment over ourselves — and at $100 a bike bag, this can get pretty expensive. Hence, much of our equipment was built in the States, and only the specialty material like time-trial bikes and special wheels came from Europe.

Because we couldn't cut any corners for the Tour DuPont, we usually needed more equipment than we did for the Tour de France. If a rider wrecked his race bike early on in a U.S. race, we couldn't just have one brought down from our home office — as we would in Europe. We needed to have one on hand to replace it. So, having at least four or five bikes for each rider was always a necessity. Furthermore, since most European teams brought the bare minimum, we always had requests from them to borrow something — so not only did we need enough equipment for us, but also for everyone else!

As all eyes were on us, everything had to be perfect — from the team cars and truck, to the bikes and our general appearance. Whether it was washing the truck or spare bikes every day, it took a little extra effort. Dealing with all the sponsors was also a lot of extra work, especially in the U.S., where there were high expectations from our American sponsors — from Motorola executives to water-bottle-cage-manufacturer representatives — to see how well their money was being spent or product used. You always had to spend a little time with each of them to keep them happy. This was not such a big deal, unless it was getting dark outside, you were missing dinner, had two more hours of work to do and your water bottle cage sponsor wanted to shoot the breeze about the day's racing.

In 1993, the team signed Volvo as a co-sponsor, supplying the team with 10 cars and three trucks. After Motorola as the team's title sponsor, Volvo's participation was one of the single most important by any company. It gave the team a fresh new look. We had the hottest team cars in bike racing, adding a lot to our team's image. Also, it was great for the staff to travel and work out of high quality vehicles. It made a huge difference to have trucks that had all the equipment and facilities that we had previously only dreamed about.

When Volvo came along they encouraged us to do a good job on the trucks, because they wanted the hottest trucks on the circuit. It was great, finally getting everything we wanted and not having to cut corners in setting them up at the beginning of the season.

When it came to preparing for the U.S. trip, I spent a lot of time talking to "Koz" — Mike Kozmatka, our U.S. warehouse manager and basic jack of all trades — about getting our truck ready. We didn't want to spend as much money on our U.S.-based truck because there were so few races there, compared to Europe; but we still needed to have the bare necessities.

I flew over to the States early, to make sure that everything would be ready on time and to give Koz a hand. He had told me that there would be a lot of work, but I assured him that with the two of us we would zip through it in no time. However, when I arrived and walked into the warehouse and surveyed what still had to be done, I quickly realized that I should have come a week earlier. For five days, I worked between 12 and 14 hours a day, slowly chipping away at the mountain of work, not taking any breaks, eating lunch while I worked, and practically running to and from the bathroom when the need arose.

The stress of those few days was incredible. It seemed like there was no way we would be ready in time. And when it finally came time to start loading the truck for my departure the next morning, I felt more tired than ever — and the race hadn't even started!

Koz had had some bike racks and wheel racks built, the latter utilizing some Yakima rack parts to save money. Everything was loaded by midnight and checked off a list for the final time to make sure nothing was forgotten. It was quite a relief to have loaded everything up, even though all the equipment wasn't quite race-ready. Then, just as I was getting ready to close the warehouse for the night, I noticed that the license plate wasn't on the truck.

"Hey, Koz, ya got a license plate for the truck?" I asked calmly, hoping this would not turn out to be a problem.

A strange look came over his face, and I panicked a little upon realizing that he didn't have it. He walked over to his desk and sat down quietly, looking through the papers, vainly attempting to find what I sensed was not there. I decided not to panic, let Koz have a few minutes to think, and continued looking through my papers to make sure everything else was ready for my departure. Everything looked to be in order, except I couldn't find the insurance card. I looked through again, and sure enough, no card.

"Hey, Koz, have you got a proof-of-insurance card for the truck?" I asked, hoping that this would not be another problem.

"I don't know, Scott," he replied with the fatigued voice of an aged retiree, riddled by the fatigue caused by the previous few days and weeks.

After spending the next two hours deciding what to do, we agreed that nothing more could be done. At 2 a.m. on Sunday, I went back to my room, feeling remarkably calm — and I couldn't figure out why. I was not going to be able to leave in the morning as planned, and would be put even further behind schedule.

The next morning, I arrived at the office at 7:30, figuring I would probably beat Koz there, but I was surprised to see him deep in conversation with someone on the phone when I arrived. Hopefully, he was getting this mess figured out.

Miraculously enough, by 9:30 a.m., it was all sorted and I said my goodbyes to Koz and our Wisconsin office. (I don't think Koz had ever been so happy to see someone leave in his whole life. His job was over, mine was just beginning. I wished it were the other way around, I thought to myself.) A few minutes later on the highway, I heard a honk and turned to see Koz give me a wave and a smile as he drove by in his Volvo on his way home. His weekend was just beginning. How envious I was of him living a "normal" life, working 9 to 5, Monday to Friday, having weekends off, being able to make plans with friends and family, going home to his own house every night after work, and having dinner with his family. The grass is always greener on the other side, I said to myself.

My first day driving was pretty uneventful. I made good progress and drove until 9 p.m. On the second day, it seemed that I would make it to Wilmington by about 3 p.m. — plenty of time to get settled at the team hotel and get a little work done.

Cresting a small hill, I saw a construction zone ahead and I naturally let up on the gas, placed my foot on the clutch pedal and hand on the gear shift, waiting slightly for the truck to slow to the appropriate speed as I applied the brake with my other foot. I pushed on the clutch pedal and prepared to change gears, but it would not move. I tried again and nothing. I looked down in disbelief just to make sure I was pushing on the right thing. I tried again in disbelief, but sure enough, it wouldn't budge and there I was, barreling down on the construction zone and going dangerously fast. I quickly stood on the brakes and I started asking myself what else I could I do?

I had to pull over, but how do you stop a 30-ton truck that's stuck in sixth gear? I had to get it into neutral, tried pushing on the clutch again as hard as I could … and finally it was moving. But not nearly enough to get it out of gear. I tried both feet, pushing as hard as I could against the seat with one foot on top of the other. It was moving! I finally got it out of gear and started looking for a place to pull over.

As I came to a stop, I wondered if the truck would get going again. I hopped out of the cab and gave it a thorough check; nothing seemed to be out of order. I was getting a little nervous — being broken down with everything for the race, and still six hours from Wilmington … not good. Where was my Motorola phone? I tried pushing in the clutch again, but after a few tries, I realized that if I used both feet and all my strength while standing on the clutch pedal, I could get it in just far enough to change gears.

In one of the numerous truck manuals was a list of all the Volvo truck dealers in North America. Hoping desperately that there would be one just over the hill, I discovered there was one 110 miles up the road. I finally got her rolling and realized quickly that I could start in second gear, rev the engine pretty high, shift to fourth and then do the same to sixth.

As I shifted into sixth, pushing with all my might and both of my feet, a loud alarm suddenly went off. I practically jumped out of my skin, looked down in shear panic, and found that the air-pressure gauge for the air brakes was dropping fast. I froze, knowing that if the pressure dropped too far that the brakes would automatically engage as a safety precaution.

My heart was racing. Were the brakes about to lock up on their own and send me careening off the road? I tried to remember from the handbook what the pressure was to engage the brakes on their own. My brow was beading with sweat at the sight of the needle on the dial suddenly stop dropping and slowly rising. Then, as I wondered what was wrong and if I could make it to the dealer, the truck slowly picked up speed; but pushing in the clutch to shift to sixth I suddenly heard the "woosh" of air escaping. It was the alarm again!

It stopped, the air gauge needle returned to normal and I realized that whenever I pushed in the clutch, air would escape. Carefully, I timed my shifts so that the air tanks fully replenished themselves before shifting again.

After what seemed like hours, I pulled off the highway and stopped for the red light at the first intersection. The alarm was sounding again, but I was used to it by this time, even though the tanks were taking too long to fill and the light was turning green before they were ready. When it turned green, all I could do was sit there and watch the gauge creep up slower than ever, while angry drivers honked at me from behind.

Finally, the alarm stopped and I made it through the intersection just as the alarm went off again and the stoplight turned red. Everyone behind me got stuck at the light again, except for the driver right behind me who immediately passed and let me know exactly what he felt.

I pulled into the Volvo dealer wondering how a brand new truck could break down, and praying that the garage mechanic could do the "wonders" that I so often did on a bicycle, to fix everything right away. Still, I knew that was pretty unlikely. I had been stuck in towns in the middle of nowhere so many times with broken-down vehicles. Once, I had to wait two days for a spare part!

Someone was watching over me again this time. The Volvo dealer mechanics weren't too busy and got me back on the road in a few hours. After trying to explain to a few of them that the Motorola team was a "bicycle" racing team, they finally convinced me to open up the back of the truck. From their reaction, you would have thought they had just seen the Grand Canyon, Niagara Falls, or even a truck full of gold bullion for the first time. However, after giving out a bunch of team hats, I was once again on my merry way, albeit wondering if I would ever reach Wilmington.

I finally hit the the the city limits when the sun set, and I smiled at the thought of all I had left in my wake since saying goodbye to Koz. And the race hadn't even started yet!

I pulled into the Holiday Inn parking lot. A few other team trucks had already set up shop in the corner. With impeccable timing, one of the U.S.-based mechanics, Sal, drove up with a car full of bikes and wheels from Atlanta.

"How was your trip?" he asked.

"Don't ask," I replied, wondering if the expression on my face told enough of the story; if not, all that I felt like explaining.

I unlocked the back of the truck so we could unload his car, and then opened the door. To my horror and utter disbelief, it was in total disarray; all the wheel racks had fallen from the wall and collapsed upon one another, crushing and throwing wheels all over the place. I cringed and dropped my face into my hands at the thought of all the work ahead — checking and fixing all those brand-new wheels and tires we had just built a few days earlier, not to mention somehow fixing the wheel rack and getting it back on the wall so we would have somewhere to store wheels for the race. It seemed that we were so far behind, we would never catch up.

So the 1994 Tour DuPont started. We worked our butts off that year, because everything that could go wrong, did. From stage one when Mexican team member Raúl Alcalá crashed and ruined the brand new bike we gave him the day before, to the end, we were always busy. When it rains it pours. A change is as good as a rest? Yeah … sure, Sean!

chapter six

The Wheel Truth
The Facts on Tires and Wheels

Lately, many people have been telling me that my job as a pro mechanic must be getting easier, what with the fact that equipment quality has improved and that bearings are all sealed. Some might feel that these improvements have cut the mechanic's responsibility to almost nothing, but the truth is that for every step forward we take with technology, we take at least a couple of steps back in other areas.

It is true now that the modern bicycle is made up entirely of sealed bearings, and that today's equipment is of much greater quality than even just a few years ago. The labor once spent in overhauling bottom brackets, hubs, headsets and pedals is pretty much gone, but this void was quickly filled by the tremendous amount of work required to carry out proper installation and maintenance of the new technologies that have replaced it.

Since the development of index shifting, for example, it has become imperative that shifting systems be in perfect working order for proper performance. The old friction shifting required little attention. There was a lever, a cable and derailleur. Now, with the advent of Shimano's STI and Campagnolo's Ergo shifters, the complexity has increased a hundred fold. Exposing all of those precise mechanisms to the rigors of European professional racing means constantly having to adjust, fine-tune and repair. New frame materials, aerodynamic equipment, multiple handlebar configurations and other innovations have made the sport faster … but added huge loads to the mechanic's responsibilities.

REINVENTING THE WHEEL

It may sound obvious, but it is true: One of the greatest developments in cycling has been the evolution of the wheel. It seems hard to imagine how you could improve so much on such a basic and simple idea, but there are more types of wheels and wheelsets available today than ever before. Besides correct bike and frame selection, wheel choice is the most important factor in determining the way your bike rides, feels, responds and performs. Assuming you have cycling shoes, clipless pedals, and a suspension fork (for a mountain bike), an upgrade in a wheelset is the single most significant improvement one can make to a bike.

It is truly amazing how noticeable nice, light, and fast wheels are. I can't tell you how often I've heard riders exclaim: "Wow! Those are fast wheels!"

New wheels not only offer a great physical advantage, but also a psychological one. If a rider thinks he has a lighter, faster bike, he will simply perform better. There is nothing worse than a rider who is demoralized by his bike. If that happens, the battle is already lost.

When I look at a wheelset to determine its value, there are four criteria by which I judge it: weight, aerodynamics, handling characteristics and durability. Depending on the type of event, each of these criteria is weighted differently. For example, in the individual time trial, aerodynamics is clearly the most important. On the other hand, in a Tour stage through the Alps, weight is the most important. For a rough and bumpy event like Paris-Roubaix, durability and handling are the primary concerns. As you can see, it is important to figure out what type of rider you are, and what type of riding you will be doing in determining which is best for you.

• DISC WHEELS A disc is the most aerodynamic type of wheel available. For individual time-trial events and triathlons they can be very beneficial. The biggest drawback of a solid disc wheel is that it has a tendency to act like a sail in windy conditions. This makes the bicycle difficult to control, and even dangerous in a strong crosswind. Discs are, therefore, used almost exclusively as rear wheels. They are occasionally used as front wheels on the track or on those rare occasions when smooth pavement and calm conditions warrant it on the road.

Most discs are quite heavy when compared with other types of wheels. Being heavier, they can be a disadvantage on hilly courses. In mass-start events, they make little sense because of the pack's constant accelerations and decelerations, and because the wheels pose a safety problem due to their relative instability in windy conditions. Because disc wheels are solid, they offer very little vertical flex or give. This reduces the amount of road shock they can absorb and increases their vertical rigidity, giving the racer a relatively harsh ride and making them hard to control. A disc is really only effective in certain conditions: flat roads and calm winds. But when those ideal conditions prevail, they can offer a significant aerodynamic advantage.

• CARBON WHEELS With carbon-fiber technology constantly improving, there has been an increase in the number and variety of spoked carbon wheels available. For many reasons, these wheels offer their biggest advantage in time trials rather than mass-start races. There are many types of these wheels available, so it is difficult to generalize about the performance of this entire category of wheels. Each type of carbon wheel must be judged on its own merits and characteristics. There are, however, some common characteristics worth mentioning. Once again let's look at our four main factors:

• WEIGHT These wheel types vary widely in weight. Some are extremely heavy, but durable; but the weight factor alone eliminates them from consideration. Some are relatively light, and have good aerodynamic qualities, but poor handling characteristics and questionable durability.

• AERODYNAMICS Almost all of these wheels have relatively good aerodynamic characteristics, but for mass-start events this is the only advantage they offer. It is difficult to understand the popularity of these wheels in mountain biking, considering that their only major apparent advantage is aerodynamic and that plays a small role at the relatively low speeds of mountain biking.

• DURABILITY All of these wheels have questionable durability in one area or another. They also suffer from the major drawback of not being repairable on the spot, like a spoked wheel.

• HANDLING CHARACTERISTICS This factor varies greatly and depends on the particular model of carbon wheel you are considering. Again, some basic rules apply. Most of those that have good lateral rigidity are pretty heavy. Those that are reasonably light have a considerable amount of lateral flex. Despite carbon's inherently good shock-absorbing characteristics, most of these wheels have to be designed to reduce lateral flex and are, therefore, stiffened in the process. Unfortunately this creates a wheel that is also vertically stiff, and that gives them a harsh ride. Instead of absorbing shock, these wheels tend to chatter and bounce over rough pavement. This reduces the amount of time the wheel is in contact with the road, and that reduces traction and makes the bike more difficult to handle.

Motorola was sponsored one season by a company that made a wheel of this type. We generally used them for time trials. However, the manufacturer was trying to break into the road market and touted them as an everyday racing and training wheel. So we were getting pressure to have our riders use them in the road races. Most of the riders didn't like them for this type of event, so it was hard to persuade them to do so. On one occasion, on the eve of the Italian season-opening classic, Milan-San Remo, Sean Yates was asked if he wouldn't mind riding these wheels in the race. Sean has always been pretty easy-going in general, and it was thought he wouldn't mind. But on the contrary, he flat-out refused. If there were anyone on the team worth listening to about the rigors of European racing, Sean was the man. He said that the final descent down the ever-crucial Poggio, just four kilometers from the finish in San Remo, was "pretty hairy," especially as it was on a bad road. Sean felt these particular wheels were too difficult to control and that they tended to "chatter" on the rough spots, and the last thing you need in a race like Milan-San Remo is anything that might hinder your performance even slightly.

The major selling feature and popularity of these wheels is the "cool" image they convey. Many people buy something because they think it is cool, like the looks of it or the way it makes them look. I'm not saying cool isn't important. It is. Cool can make the difference between someone enjoying something, or not. Often, in a recreational pursuit, that can be the bottom line. However, from a performance perspective, most of these wheels suffer from some disadvantage or another when compared with spoked wheels. So keep that in mind.

SPOKED WHEELS

There is a huge variety of spoked wheels out there. Whether you're building a pair of bomb-proof training wheels or buying a pair of deep-section, high-performance race wheels, you still need to ask yourself what kind of riding you plan to do and under what conditions you plan to use the wheels.

Deep-section aero' rims come in a variety of profiles. The taller the rim, the more aerodynamic your finished wheel will be. Deeper rims will also be stronger and, because of that, you can get away with using fewer spokes. That, in turn, will improve the wheel's aerodynamic qualities. They are usually made from aluminum alloy and carbon fiber. Of course, while carbon rims are considerably lighter, they are a lot more expensive.

Pre-built wheelsets are offered with as few as 16 spokes, most often laced radially with bladed spokes and although not super-light, very aerodynamic. These wheelsets can be relatively light and strong, because they are designed as a single unit and not from a mix of unrelated components.

Some of the better carbon rims come with an aluminum braking surface or side wall, which is always an important factor to consider. A braking surface not only provides better and more consistent braking, particularly in wet conditions, but the wheel tends to react better to heavy impacts, by denting instead of cracking or chipping. It is therefore much easier to repair. Aluminum rims often feature machined or ceramic-coated surfaces to enhance braking.

If you are looking for lightweight rims, then the sky is the limit. However, you should remember that most people are a little too preoccupied with weight savings these days. It is easy to go overboard in the search for gram-saving equipment. To me, it seems that among some racers there is almost as much competition in the search for the lightest bike as there is in a sprint finish. Frankly, most people would be better served by dropping a pound or two of body weight than by spending a fortune to trim a pound from their bikes. When looking for wheels, durability is a very important factor to consider, as is weight, but if it doesn't get you to the finish line it isn't worth it.

That said, it is true that the most significant weight savings on a bicycle are those made by changing your wheels. Every acceleration, whether it be from a stop light or in a field sprint, requires you to bring your body weight and bicycle up to speed by making your wheels spin faster. Imagine holding a super-light road wheel in your hand and spinning it as hard as you can. Think of doing the same with a heavy disc. It requires much more effort and energy to get a disc wheel to spin at the same speed as the light wheel, because of the added weight. The same happens when riding.

When building a set of light wheels keep in mind that light rims need more spokes (like 32 or 36) than heavier stronger rims. It is also better to err on the heavier side than the lighter side, because it doesn't matter how light equipment is, if it doesn't get a rider to the finish line.

Many people ask if someone who weighs 180 pounds can ride a light set of wheels. That's the wrong question. I've known plenty of big riders who are quite easy on equipment and smaller racers who can tear up almost anything you put under them. Proper wheel choice really depends on riding style. Does the racer have a good position on the bike? Is he or she strong? And, most importantly, what's his or her bike-handling ability?

Some people are naturally much better on a bicycle than others. They simply have more finesse, are easier on their bikes and can get away with more delicate equipment. Steve Bauer, who has always done well in classics like Paris-Roubaix, very rarely flatted, crashed or wrecked wheels because he was such a good bike handler and didn't damage equipment. Lance Armstrong, a very, very strong rider, usually used more brute force than finesse and tended to power through moments when in trouble. This could be why early in his career, Lance never had good results and very few finishes in the cobbled classics like the Tour of Flanders — he would rarely make it to the finish trouble-free!

LACING OPTIONS

A number of different spoking patterns are used today. Since the invention of the modern bicycle wheel, the good old "three-cross" pattern has been the industry standard. Three-cross refers to the number of times an individual spoke crosses other spokes between the rim and hub. I would guess that as many as 99 percent of bicycle wheels on the road or trail still use this pattern. However, radial lacing — in which the spoke travels directly from hub to rim, without crossing any other spokes — has really taken off in the last few years, and has now become the standard on many high-end bikes.

When I joined up with the Motorola team, radial lacing was rarely used. If it was, it was usually only on time-trial wheels. I was a big advocate of this type of wheel, and I finally persuaded the head mechanic to use them more often on the road. By the end of that first year, Motorola was using them with great success.

Spoked wheels seem like a relatively simple piece of equipment, but they can be very complex. A wheel is constantly undergoing different stresses, whether from the drivetrain, or lateral stresses as the rider moves the bicycle from side to side while out of the saddle, or simply from the constant flexing and absorption of impact from the road.

A well-built wheel should offer lateral rigidity for better performance and absorb enough road shock to offer a comfortable ride by being somewhat vertically flexible under impact and vibration. A three-cross wheel, unless tensioned very tight, will usually absorb more road shock and be a little more forgiving than a radial-laced wheel, because the spokes will flex more against one another, than on a radial wheel. These wheels are also more appropriate for touring and races like Paris-Roubaix where shock absorption is crucial. A radial wheel, however, is generally stiffer and slightly lighter, because the spokes are shorter and more aerodynamic, resulting in a better wheel for the high-performance cyclist, not to mention that they-look cool.

For the Tour DuPont one year, Motorola had some 32-hole wheels built with radially laced bladed spokes — front and rear — on aero' rims. They weighed a ton. Still, trying to talk Lance Armstrong out of riding them was impossible. There was a hilly stage the next day and he would have been better off using a lighter set. The new and heavier ones could have been saved for a flatter stage, but he wouldn't hear of it. He wanted to ride them because he thought they were the latest and coolest out there.

Having a too-stiff wheel, particularly vertically stiff, is less of a concern in mountain biking than on the road. Mountain bikes have large tires run at a lower pressure that absorb considerable shock before it even enters the wheel. On the road a high-pressure 20mm tire offers little or no suspension. These days, most mountain bikes also come equipped with suspension forks. For both those reasons, radial lacing is the ideal spoke pattern for mountain bikes.

TIRES

The choice of tire is almost as complicated as choosing the right type of wheel. It is certainly one of the most important factors, since tires are the only part of the bicycle to make contact with the ground. Road cyclists also have to consider the choice between tubulars (sew-ups) and clinchers.

• TUBULARS A tubular tire is one in which the tube is sewn into a nylon, cotton or silk casing (hence, the name "sew-up"). A base tape is then applied over the stitches to provide a smooth surface for gluing the tire to the rim. Tubulars have been the most widely used type of tire used on road bikes, especially in competition.

There are advantages and disadvantages with tubular tires. First, from a performance standpoint, a tubular has much better riding and handling characteristics than even the best clinchers. Comparisons between tubulars and clinchers of the same diameter will show that tubulars are much nicer, easier riding tires and have a much better feel to them than clinchers do. Not surprisingly, they are tires of choice for most professional cyclists. However, there are still some great disadvantages with tubulars. While proper installation of a tubular is not difficult, it is crucial to the safety of the rider. The process requires constant attention to make certain that the glue has not dried out and that the tire is still secure on the rim.

The risk of "rolling" a tire is one of a mechanic's greatest nightmares. Even the most carefully mounted tubular can roll off. For example, when a rider clips a pedal while negotiating a corner, the rear wheel can lift off the ground and come down at an angle. The shear force, combined with the weight and centrifugal force of the rider as he accelerates out of the corner, can roll almost any tubular tire, no matter how well it has been installed. This has happened many times and, while it is the rider's fault when it does, everyone looks at the mechanic as if it were his fault.

For any mechanic working on a professional team, it takes a lot of time and energy to regularly inspect every wheel in the team arsenal. The time needed to glue on a tubular is far greater than that needed for simply popping on a clincher. That extra time can add up when you need to mount 40 tires in one day, not to mention the next day's careful inspections and scraping of excess glue.

Even with all of that attention, there is still always something that gnaws at the back of your mind when you see your riders screaming down a descent in the Alps, reaching speeds up to 110 kph (not to mention the fear of riders from other teams whose mechanic just might have missed something). Living in fear that a tire might roll, you find yourself always wondering if each wheel has been closely checked. One of the greatest drawbacks of a tubular in top-level racing is that as the rim heats up from the accumulation of breaking at high speed on long steep descents, and the glue begins to melt, the tire can creep or start to "turn" on the rim. The tread rolls to the side and all of a sudden you're riding on side wall. That tire will eventually roll off. Even if it doesn't at that point, quite often as the glue heats up, it is squeezed out the sides of the tire, leaving very little of anything for the tire to adhere to the next day.

Some riders are naturally much better on descents than others and will never have a problem of tires creeping, because they brake so little. For riders like Sean Yates, descending is all about "driving" the bicycle, being a part of it and allowing it to descend at speed and with the flow of the race. Cyclists like Sean are as comfortable screaming down a mountain descent at more than 100 kph as they are sitting on the couch at home watching a ball game on television. They can race on tubulars with very little danger of tires creeping, while others will always be relegated to using clinchers in the mountains because they are terrible descenders. They brake far too often, and so increase the risk of tire creep.

Even seasoned pros sometimes use clinchers in the mountains purely for safety reasons. Five-time Tour de France winner Miguel Indurain almost always rode clinchers in the mountains in the big tours.

Another obvious disadvantage of tubulars is that they are expensive. A good tubular should run you at least $60, and considering that there is no guarantee it will not puncture in the first kilometer on the road, this can make for an expensive tire choice. Once a tubular punctures, it is better to simply trash it, unlike a clincher which can be easily repaired. (If you do repair a tubular, it should be used only for training, not racing.) And, last but not least, as the quality standards of many tubular manufacturers have gone downhill in recent years, trying to find a good value-for-money tubular is a crap shoot.

The choice to use tubulars is a questionable one, even in top-level racing; but if you do decide to follow this route make sure they are installed by an experienced mechanic. These days it is not so uncommon to find a bike shop mechanic who has never glued one on before. For my very first pair of tubular racing wheels, the tires were installed by a mechanic who had never done it before. In that case, the tires were quite secure, but there was glue all over the place. It was a mess.

INSTALLING A TUBULAR TIRE

- When gluing a tubular, make sure you are in a well-ventilated area.
- Clean the rim with mineral spirits or thinner, and wipe dry.
- Rough up the surface of the rim with a file to give the glue a good surface to adhere to.
- Some professional mechanics file the eyelets down slightly to give a smoother, flatter surface for the tire to stick to. However, this isn't vital, as it will most likely void the warranty on your rim.
- It is almost impossible to avoid a lump at the valve once the tire is mounted, because the tire enlarges slightly at the base of the valve, making the tire sit higher at this spot. Most rims have a slightly larger valve hole on the outer section of the rim to help this problem. Some don't, and drilling out the outer section only to 8mm to 10mm will help this problem. Clean off any filings that are left.
- Apply a thin coat of glue to the rim, making sure to cover the entire surface, especially the edges. Let it dry overnight if possible.
- Pump enough air into the tire to give it some shape, but not so much that it starts to turn inside out.
- Stretch the tire a little by placing both hands on either side of the valve, with your foot on the opposite side of the tire; stretch it for a few seconds. Be sure not to pull so hard that you rip the base tape.
- Most tires come with a clear protective coating over the casing and base tape preventing the glue from being absorbed into the base tape. It is necessary to either scrape this coating off with a blade, or clean it with mineral spirits. If using mineral spirits, be careful not to use too much otherwise it will soak through and break down the glue adhering the base tape to the casing.
- Apply a coat of glue to the tire, making sure to get the edges, and let it dry. If the base tape is very absorbent, a second coat is not a bad idea.
- At this point you can either apply two more thin coats to the rim,

or one medium coat before mounting. If it is a new rim, the application of two thin coats is better. Let the first of the two coats dry a little and get tacky before applying the second.

- You now have two options. You may either mount the tire right away, or wait for the last rim coat to get tacky. If you mount it while it is wet, there is a better chance of moving the tire on the rim to get it straight; but if you wait for the glue to get tacky it will set more firmly and require less time to dry. It will, however, be difficult to move on the rim if you don't get it perfectly placed the first try.

- To mount the tire, balance the wheel at your feet in front of you with the valve hole pointing straight up at you; make sure the tire has enough air in it to give it shape and firmness, and grasp it at both sides of the valve, stretch it and insert the valve into the valve hole. Make sure that it's straight, and slowly work your way down around to the bottom of the tire, while stretching it the whole time and applying even amounts of pressure to it and making sure that the tire is going on straight.

- When you get to the last 8 to 10 inches, lift and push the rest of the tire over the edge of the rim, making sure not to smear glue onto the side wall. It is important to apply an even amount of pressure on the tire while stretching it on, and not just the last part. Otherwise, you will end up with a lumpy tire with high and low spots in it.

- Pump the tire up to about 75-percent pressure. Don't pump it to full pressure, otherwise if the glue is wet the tire might try to creep and turn and possibly prevent itself from seating down into the rim.

- Make sure that an even amount of base tape is showing on either side and that the tire is straight.

- Spin the tire in a truing stand and make sure the tire is straight and not too lumpy. If it is, try to work the lumps out if the glue is wet, but the effort is very difficult and usually a waste of time.

- Now that the tire is straight, and hopefully evenly proportioned around the rim, roll the wheel along the ground while applying pressure to the top. This squeezes the tire and rim together and distributes the glue evenly into any gaps.

• There are two ways to clean the excess glue off the rim. Usually, if you are experienced at mounting tires, there won't be very much and scraping it off with a razor blade the next day will do the trick. But you can also clean the rim with a rag and mineral spirits right after mounting, if you are careful not to use too much and get it on the tire. Be sure to wipe off any excess. Well, after all that, a nice pair clinchers doesn't sound so bad, does it?

CLINCHERS

Most bikes are equipped with clincher tires. Clincher tires come in two separate parts: the tube and the tire. Unlike tubulars, the tire is attached to the rim by means of hook beads on both sides of the tire that fit into the grooves of the rim. They are simple to install, reasonably priced and there are all types available.

Unlike the lengthy process of installing a tubular, putting on a clincher is quick, doesn't leave a mess and can be done by anyone after just a few minutes of instruction. While a clincher's condition should be checked regularly, inspections are not quite as critical as they are on tubulars. And while the performance of even the best clinchers is slightly inferior to that of a tubular, the difference has gotten so small over the past few years that it is really no longer an issue. Even in that it is not worth making it a concern.

Clinchers are no longer the old, heavy, poor-handling products of years ago. Indeed some look identical to tubulars and can only be spotted through close inspection by a well-trained eye. Look, for example, at all of the photos of Indurain racing and try to spot the clinchers. It is tough, even though he used them almost exclusively in the mountains.

There is one large disadvantage to using clinchers. Fortunately, this doesn't happen very often, but when a blowout occurs, the tire becomes instantly flat with no air remaining in the tire. When this happens with a clincher, the tire can come completely off the rim, leaving the unlucky cyclist riding on the bare rim. The tire depends on air pressure to secure itself to the rim, whereas a tubular tire does not, and will stay on the rim giving the cyclist some traction to get the bike under control. This rare phenomenon can be especially disastrous on descents.

There are advantages and disadvantages to both types of tires, but it is safe to say that clinchers are the better choice for most applications.

Many riders, like Lance Armstrong, prefer training on big, fat, heavy clinchers. They provide a softer ride and add a little resistance to their training. When race day rolls around, the bike feels much lighter and faster with a pair of race wheels installed. A larger tire is also less prone to flatting because of the lower pressures needed in them. The tire is more pliable and puncture-resistant to sharp debris, and less prone to pinch flats, because the tire is larger in diameter. Motorola used very large diameter tubular tires for races like Paris-Roubaix. The idea was to provide more traction in wet conditions, as tire pressure decreased. Tubulars are also more resistant to pinch flats, a characteristic that improves as tire diameter increases. Tubulars are a good choice for the cobbles of Roubaix. Still, the race has been won on clinchers, most recently by Frédéric Guesdon in 1997.

There are now also new tire materials that can make things a little more interesting. Besides having the traditional black-rubber compound, a few manufacturers have come out with a range of weather-specific tires. Vittoria makes a wet-weather tire that features a roughened black center and green sides, made of a softer rubber compound to give better traction in wet weather and for cornering. When completely upright, the tire's normal black tread is in contact with the pavement, but when cornering calls for greater traction, the softer green tread takes over. The dry-weather tires are slightly smaller in diameter and have a smooth tread, giving them slightly less rolling resistance. They are primarily used for time trailing or road races with good roads in dry conditions.

The real advantage of multi-compound tires is questionable, except under extreme conditions like Paris-Roubaix. They really are more for show, and serve as a way for the tire manufacturer to sell more tires. Any manufacturer's goal is to grow, and a major way to do that is by introducing new and improved products, but there are limits as to what can be developed in the bicycle component and accessory industry. Look at handlebars. How can handlebars be further improved? How many new models can be introduced every year? It is the same with tires, but then manufacturers will keep on trying. And as long as they come out with new equipment, salespeople will always be there to push the product to consumers. So be wary and use a little common sense when listening to the sales pitch on the latest wonder product, whatever it might be.

Once, I met a guy at the bike shop who hadn't done much riding, but had recently bought his first real mountain bike. He had come to love cycling so much that he was in the process of upgrading several parts on his bike. Partially from recommendations of various salespeople, he had upgraded his derailleurs, shifters, brakes, handlebars and stem. On this particular day, he planned to spend a chunk of cash to upgrade his crankarms. Meanwhile, he was still riding the same mediocre wheelset that had originally come with the bike.

It shocked and frustrated me that the salespeople had led him in this direction and convinced him that these were the right areas to focus upon. It wasn't that he was buying the top-of-the-line cranks, he was simply upgrading one component group level of Shimano cranks. I certainly couldn't blame him. He had just been introduced to the sport and didn't know much about anything. It seemed that either the salespeople didn't have a clue, as well, or they just wanted to make a quick buck.

A good wheelset will make a bigger difference in the overall performance of a bicycle than anything else, maybe even more than all other possible upgrades combined. Next to the frame, wheels are what determines the way a bicycle feels, handles, climbs, corners, accelerates and responds. Having a bike on which you feel comfortable and enjoy riding is the key to success and enjoyment in the sport. Having a good pair of wheels with nice tires will not only enhance that enjoyment, but will give cyclists every opportunity to reach their full potential.

chapter seven

The Greatest Race:
The Tour de France

Le Tour de France, *La Grande Boucle* or, simply, the Tour. Whatever you call it, it's still the biggest of the big races, the granddaddy of them all. The *maillot jaune* — the yellow leader's jersey — of the Tour is the most coveted prize in international cycling. Nothing else compares. For the Italians, the Giro d'Italia is important; and for the Spanish, the Vuelta a España is the priority; but for everyone, the Tour de France is the pinnacle.

The Tour is the only race in which only the very best riders of the very best teams are invited to compete. Unless you've been to the event, it's hard to explain what separates the Tour from all the other races. Whatever it is, it's reflected in the nervous excitement that you see in everyone's eyes. And for anyone who works in the sport, it's the ultimate dream to "do" the Tour de France. It was certainly my dream to be a part of it.

I worked as a mechanic on the Tour four times and have many memories. Thankfully, they're mostly good memories. But whether drinking champagne and toasting a victory or fighting back tears after a tragedy, the many ups and downs are what make the Tour de France so memorable.

First meetings often leave the strongest impressions. Such was the case with my introduction to the Tour in 1992. In fact, even before the race, just knowing that I was finally about to realize something I had only dreamed about gave me goose bumps. The race was due to start in San Sebastian, in northern Spain, and beforehand we had to set up a team time trial training camp at St. Emilion, just outside of Bordeaux. So St. Emilion — a prime center of the region's wine country — was our destination when I and the team's head soigneur, John Hendershot, left Motorola's team headquarters in Belgium. We had been warned by Noël Dejonckheere, our Belgian operations manager and a former professional cyclist, that a truck drivers' strike in France might make it difficult to travel on the *autoroute*. What an understatement!

Driving a team car, we were soon in France and within half an hour reached Lille — and hit the first traffic jam. In the next hour, we moved less than a mile. The truck drivers had completely shut down the *autoroute*, lining the road four abreast and moving only a few feet every few minutes. After listening to the radio, I realized that this was going on all over the country, shutting down all travel into and out of Paris and throughout France.

As an American it was hard to understand this countrywide protest — because things like that just don't happen in the States. Americans wouldn't put up with it. But here, I saw drivers standing outside their vehicles, smoking cigarettes, laughing and talking with the police ... and the protesters!

Finally, after a couple of hours, we made it to an exit from the highway, took the back roads and returned home to Belgium. Two other staff members were scheduled to leave for St. Emilion the next morning, so we decided to all leave together at 4 a.m. After taking six hours to reach to Paris — for what should have been a two-and-a-half-hour drive — we picked up the four official team Fiats for the Tour.

We eventually arrived in St. Emilion at 11 p.m., having taken twice as long as we should have ... and immediately hit the bar. We got up early the next morning and prepared the riders' time-trial bikes for their training ride on the course they would race on a week later. I went with Jim Ochowicz in the team car, in case anyone needed adjustments or mechanical tweaks to their bikes. We drove the course once with the riders in the cars, as I struggled to stay awake. I kept thinking that it was a waste of time driving over the course like this. Why not just put them on their bikes and have them ride it?

Finally, we stopped. I unloaded the bikes and they rode off, with Jim and me following in one car, and Hennie Kuiper in the other. After a short warm-up, it soon became clear why we did drive the course first. The riders, wanting to get a real feel for all the corners and terrain, gradually picked up the pace to what they would ride in the Tour. I had never seen a full nine-man team time trial like this before, and I soon realized why so much importance was placed on this one event. Watching them, I was getting a little nervous — which is unusual for me. It seemed like they were riding at the limit, and I kept thinking someone was going to overlap a wheel and fall.

A crash in the team time trial is a mechanic's worst nightmare, and I was becoming aware of this very quickly. If someone crashes, they could take everyone else down with them, and at that speed it could be disastrous. What would you do if seven riders were lying on the ground in a heap of broken equipment while the clock is ticking? That's why a team time trial is the single most stressful event for a team mechanic. I always looked forward to it, as there is nothing more impressive than seeing nine riders from the same team racing flat out only centimeters apart in one long line. But I was always more than glad when it was over.

It really takes a brilliant display of team cohesion to win the team time trial at the Tour. Some riders can go too hard, and make the others suffer. And in most cases, riders try harder than in any other event, because of not wanting to let down the team. If one is dropped and the team doesn't wait, it's very likely he won't make the time limit and will be automatically disqualified from the race. That's not a nice prospect in the first week of the Tour; and so some riders, suffering like dogs to stay with the others, lose control and start riding erratically. That's when crashes can occur.

The team time trial is one of the most prestigious stages to win at the Tour, because it's a reflection on each team's ability and its teamwork. That's why it was so important that Motorola always tried to win the TTT. The team may have lacked superstars like Indurain, but it always prided itself on trying to at least make an impact on each Tour — and doing well in the team time trial was the ideal way to start.

After a couple of days in St. Emilion, we drove on to San Sebastian. I was immediately impressed with the whole Tour scene. It was unlike any race I had ever been at. Our team had three mechanics, four soigneurs, a helper, a doctor, a cook, two public relations officers, two team directors, and a representative from Motorola — plus 10 bike riders (one extra in case someone got sick or hurt at the last minute). That the team flew in an extra rider just to be on call reflected the importance of this race above all the others, and it made me realize that I was now in the big league. What a production: twenty-five people on the Motorola Tour de France team, and I was finally one of them!

Willy Balmat, the team cook, was from Switzerland. He met Jim Ochowicz on a flight in Europe years earlier, and the two hit it off immediately. Willy is one of the wildest and most high-energy people I've met, besides of course being a world-class chef. Sometimes, after we had finished working on the bikes, I would go into the kitchen and help him prepare dinner, to pick up a few tips. Some of my best recipes are thanks to Willy.

Getting fed on time is one of the riders' biggest problems at a race — particularly if you are in a hotel with 10 other teams, and all 100 bike riders want to be fed at the same time. This can be one of the most stressful times for the soigneurs, whose prime goal is to make sure the riders are fed as fast as possible. So having Willy on hand was a blessing for everyone on the team. He always went into the kitchen, talked to the hotel's head chef and basically made sure everyone was fed right away — and well! Some mornings, if you were up early enough and Willy was in a good mood, he would even cook the staff fried eggs and ham. I'm not a big fried eggs fan, but to this day I have never had fried eggs and ham like Willy's.

The day of the prologue is hectic for mechanics. A time trial demands a tremendous amount of work, because of the organization needed to make sure everything goes smoothly. There is an incredible amount of special equipment required for this one day, and the pressure on a mechanic to ensure that there are no problems is relentless. The clock ticks constantly on prologue day, from the moment we wake up until the time we hit the hay late at night.

In the morning, we prepared the time-trial bikes for the riders to train on, so they could get used to them and there would be enough time to make adjustments for the late-afternoon prologue. While they trained, we prepared their road bikes for the following day's road race, and the spare bikes and wheels for the prologue.

At that first Tour, I was overwhelmed by the amount of equipment lying around — there was stuff everywhere. When the riders returned, we made the changes they wanted, gave their bikes a quick wipe down, and installed the appropriate wheels and gave them a thorough check. It was clear how important it is for the mechanics to work together. There was so much to do, and so little time, and we each had to give 100-percent concentration to the task at hand.

When it was time to go to the prologue start, the only job I had to finish was preparing Phil Anderson's bike for the next day's road stage. It didn't seem a problem. I thought I could do it after the prologue. (At the Tour, or any big stage race, each mechanic is responsible for the same bikes throughout the entire race, because familiarity with a bike remains with the mechanic who has been working on it every day. It's more efficient not having to check over some of the things you know you've checked the day before.)

I'll never forget the first few moments after arriving at the start of my first Tour prologue. All the people, the excitement, the noise of the team cars and motorcycles whizzing by and horns blasting … it was truly incredible. I had finally made it to the Tour de France.

I tried not to look too excited going about my duties to help riders with whatever they needed, while keeping an eye on all the equipment and team cars. Neil Lacey, the other mechanic that year, and I decided that he would follow the first group of Motorola riders, and I would follow the second. So I stayed by the team car to help the riders and give their tires a quick check, to make sure their tires hadn't picked up any glass or been damaged in their warm-up.

Soon, the Motorola team car pulled up and Lacey hopped out, yelling to me: "Your turn!" I obliged, jumped in the car and followed another rider, driving into a mass of controlled hysteria. I had never seen such huge crowds at a bike race: The fans stood 10 deep at the start, and crowds were thick all around the 8km course. Not one spot was free for any latecomers!

The day went without incident and we arrived back at the hotel before dinner. With the day's sensations now subsiding, hunger pangs took over my inclination to do more work. As he put away the last bike, George Noyes asked me, "Do you want to mount Phil's bike?"

"Aahh, he can do it in the morning," answered Neil Lacey.

George looked at me, and I said: "I can do it in the morning, no problem."

As I thought it over, I recalled having given Anderson's bike a quick check before training that morning. Mounting his bike the next day seemed okay to me.

"All right, it's up to you," said George, finally locking up the truck while I looked forward to a moment of self-congratulation for completing the first day of my first Tour de France….

The next morning, after a quick breakfast of bread and Spanish coffee, I and the other Motorola mechanics went out to the truck and began a routine that would be repeated every day for the next three weeks. After all the cars were washed, we opened the truck and Noyes and Lacey began unloading all the equipment, while I worked on Anderson's bike. I was about to put the wheels in when I stopped to check the bottom bracket. I removed the chain and spun the cranks, while holding the seat tube just above the front derailleur, and listened. It was in bad shape. Spinning it again, I looked down at my watch to see how much time there was before it was time to leave for the start. A jolt of panic shot through my veins as I realized that I hadn't checked Anderson's bottom bracket the day before when I had the chance. Here it was, in really bad shape, and I had only 25 minutes before the team was due to leave. Still, I thought there was enough time, and jumped up into the truck to grab a new bottom bracket from the spare-parts drawer and began my supposed wizardry.

"What's up?" asked Lacey.

"His bottom bracket is trashed!" I replied.

"Hey, we don't have time for that right now!" said Lacey, pointing at his watch.

"I can do it!" I said, starting to get a little irritated at losing a few precious seconds with this debate, when George intervened, saying: "No, I don't want you rushing that, besides we have other things to do."

George was the boss, so I finished Phil's bike, not having replaced the bottom bracket and being a little annoyed for not having been able to. We got everything done and loaded just as the riders came down and hopped in the cars for a short drive to the start.

The stage — out and back from San Sebastian — was pretty uneventful, until the 50km-to-go sign, when the voice on the race radio shouted: "Motorola! Motorola!" I shot up in my seat, the adrenaline pumping through my veins. The race had just started going flat-out, with the sprinters' teams anxious to make their first strike at winning a stage. Being in the second car with Hennie Kuiper, my hands were tied as I waited for some word over the radio from Jim Ochowicz in the first car. It wasn't a long wait....

"Hennie! Can you come up, we had to give Phil his spare bike!"

I nearly went through the roof, dying to grab the radio and find out what the problem was. I knew it wasn't the time to pursue it, so I tried to keep calm, not wanting anyone who might be listening to the radio realize what had happened if it had been my fault. It was the longest 50km of my life. I couldn't wait to get to the finish, to find out what had happened.

Finally, after the finish, I leapt from the car and walked up to Neil trying to appear nonchalant about the whole thing, "What happened to Phil's bike?" I asked, as if mildly curious.

"His bottom bracket blew up," replied Neil, realizing the full impact of his words.

"Shit! I told George it needed to be overhauled!" I was so angry. I had hoped something like this would *never* happen, let alone on the first day of the Tour. I was fuming. By the end of the night, everyone on the team would know that it was *my* bike that had failed. I felt I had let the team down. Here was my first real chance to show everyone that I had earned the right to be here with the best of the best, and the first day I blew it! I knew it would take a long time to earn back that trust and respect. When we arrived back at the hotel I was so angry, particularly at George for not letting me replace it that morning, when I knew it needed replacing.

I learned a valuable lesson from that episode ... although it took me a long time to realize it. Months later, I realized that George had been right in not letting me repack Phil's bottom bracket that morning. It had been entirely my fault, since Phil's bike was my responsibility. I shouldn't have left it for that morning, but finished it the night before — unless I was 110-percent confident that it was race-ready. My over-confidence and caving in to peer pressure — not to mention my dinner-desperate stomach at the time — had been my downfall.

George's only fault may have been his decision to take a mechanic with such obvious weaknesses — me — to the most important race of the year. It wasn't a question of whether I could have replaced the bottom bracket in the time I had, but how much of a disaster would have occurred had I failed. Can you imagine the situation had I encountered a problem while Phil's bottom bracket was lying in pieces, and the team was ready to leave for the race?

It took me a long time to become a good professional mechanic. When I say "professional," I not only mean working for a pro team, but being a mechanic who goes about his job in a truly professional manner, and instills confidence in his riders and fellow team members — not one who thinks he knows everything, and then screws up.

MY TOUR DIARY

In 1995, I kept a daily diary of what happened to me and the team — from fantastically good to tragically bad. However, for me, the rigors of the Tour began well before its July 1 start at St Brieuc in the Brittany region of France. The days leading up to the Tour can be some of the busiest and most stressful of the season — a constant game of catch-up, building bikes and wheels for the upcoming events. That year, after a mad dash back to Belgium from the Tour of Catalonia stage race in Spain, there were long hours of bike- and wheel-building, and double checking every list....

June 27 It's an early start, prompted by the excitement of finally leaving for the start of the Tour. After a quick breakfast, I check the office for any overnight faxes, load the final items in the truck, and hit the road.

An eight-hour drive leads me to our quaint, family-run hotel in the French countryside, in time to get the truck set up for the weeks ahead. We are staying near the team time trial course at Mayenne for a couple of days, close enough so the riders can acquaint themselves with what will be the Tour's third stage. After debating whether to work on the bikes, the pressure of the preceding days and what lies ahead get the better of me. A beer with one of our soigneurs, Freddy Viaene, seems like a better alternative, while we wait for the riders to arrive. When they do, we load all their bikes in the truck, unload the team cars, and call it a day.

June 28   I wake up at 6:30. After breakfast, it's time to unload bikes from the truck and prepare them for the day's training — a process that becomes as much of a habit as cleaning your teeth every morning. There are a lot of bikes to prepare: time-trial bikes for team time trial practice, as well as the road bikes, because the riders want to ride back to the hotel on them afterward. That means loading and preparing 20 bikes in all.

That's not to mention our work on three new Lotus bikes I built in the last few days. They have to be finished and positioned for their riders. Then it's time to wash all the spare bikes and mount (install wheels and check them over), and prepare a few of the riders' spare time-trial bikes for the prologue. Most of the riders request enough changes to keep me busy until dinner time.

June 29   After preparing the bikes for training, John Hendershot and I drive for four hours to our first official Tour hotel … only to be confronted with a local flea market that blocks the street. We have to wait more than an hour to move the last half-mile to the hotel, and then carefully make our way through the rabble, reluctantly accepting the dirty looks and shouts from the angry French market vendors, who'd prefer that we wait until they are all packed up.

Things don't get any better once we reach the hotel. Parking is not ideal, particularly as we need space for two trucks to facilitate switching and reorganizing the bikes and wheels from one to the other. After an hour, a few spaces open up across the street from the hotel, right on the quayside of the small fishing port. The only problem is that a car is blocking the last spot needed to get the truck in. After losing three valuable work hours, I grab Shot and Freddy, and we physically bounce the car over a parking space. The truck fits in nicely!

The riders arrive at 6 p.m., and George with the other truck at 7:30. We reorganize a few bikes, change a few saddles and finally pack up at 8:45 p.m. — in time to grab a shower, have dinner and hit the sack.

June 30 I wake up 6:30 (again!), get the bikes ready for training (again!), and most riders want to ride both their time trial and road bikes (again!). The day is spent preparing for tomorrow's race — gluing on tires, washing bikes, and then mounting spare and time trial bikes for the race when the riders return.

July 1 The riders are out training by 9:30 to check out the prologue course. When they return, we have to change their handlebars and gears and get all the bikes race-ready. After lunch, I load up the time-trial bikes, and leave for the prologue course. Sunny weather greets us, but clouds start rolling in and threaten rain — which may be a potential problem, because the Lotus bikes have dry-weather tires.

Our first three starters — Kaspars Ozers, Frankie Andreu and Steve Swart — ride without a problem. It is still dry, but just as Fabio Casartelli prepares to start, rain begins falling heavily and the wind picks up. He almost crashes, as does Steve Bauer, who is our next rider off. As the wind increases, barriers along the finishing straight blow over, and Bauer can barely keep his bike upright.

We haven't expected the weather to turn on us like this, and we aren't really prepared. We don't have enough non-dry-weather tires for the wet streets, or spoked front wheels to combat the strong wind. I try to convince Lance Armstrong not to use a disc wheel on the rear because of the wind, but he decides to anyway. The whole thing is quite a mess — trying to take wheels from guys who have finished for guys who are waiting to start. Bikes are transferred back and forth, from one car to the other in pouring rain.

Miraculously, the rest of the guys get through okay, even though the weather remains terrible. It's still a disappointing day, though, as the riders can't really give it their best. Those who went off first have the best times, particularly those on the Castorama team, which was smart enough to place a few of its good riders early in the starting order, in anticipation of the bad weather. Their reward is clear: a first place and the yellow leader's jersey for Jacky Durand, and second place for Thierry Laurent. For us, Frankie Andreu is the best placed, in seventh position, followed by Swart in ninth.

Prologue: St. Brieuc-St. Brieuc, 7.3km

1. Jacky Durand (F), Castorama; 2. Thierry Laurent (F), Castorama; 3. Francis Moreau (F), GAN.

July 2 Rain threatens again, so we change all the wheels on the race bikes to rain tires — a time-costing process that is only adding to the stress we already feel after the prologue. As a result, we arrive at the stage start in Dinan a little later than everyone else.

The stage gives a prime opportunity for Frankie to make up his five-second overall deficit and take the yellow jersey from Durand. Unfortunately, he just isn't fast enough. In fact, most of the other teams have the same idea, and as a result every intermediate sprint that offers time bonuses becomes highly competitive. Frankie does earn one two-second bonus and moves up to fifth overall, but he is still five seconds behind. The rain starts after only 20km, and the ensuing crashes and punctures don't make things any easier for us.

Thankfully, the hotel is close to the finish. We wash all the spare bikes and wheels, as well as the race bikes, because the rain made them filthy. However, having three mechanics at the race for the first time doesn't appear to be much of a help — at least to begin with — because it makes getting into a groove pretty hard.

Stage 1: Dinan—Lannion, 233.5km

1. Fabio Baldato (I), MG-Technogym; 2. Laurent Jalabert (F), ONCE; 3. Djamolidin Abdujaparov (Uzb), Novell.

Overall: 1. Durand; 2. Laurent Brochard (F), Festina; 3. Laurent Jalabert.

July 3 Another sprinter's race sees Frankie drop to 10th place overall, at 27 seconds. I travel in the first car with Och and my only action is when Ozers has a rear flat. After washing the bikes at the hotel, we mount the team time trial bikes for tomorrow. The disc wheels we have been waiting for arrive late. Realizing that we don't have freewheels for them, the discs are useless anyway. But then the riders surprise us by all choosing regular-spoked front wheels, as opposed to three-spoke wheels. It's an unusual choice and one we aren't quite prepared for.

Stage 2: Perros-Guirec—Vitré, 235.5km

1. MARIO CIPOLLINI (I), MERCATONE UNO-SAECO; 2. GIOVANNI LOMBARDI (I), LAMPRE-PANARIA; 3. ABDUJAPAROV.

Overall: 1. JALABERT; 2. BROCHARD; 3. BRUNO THIBOUT (F), CASTORAMA.

July 4 The team is training on team time trial bikes by 10 a.m. On returning, Lance Armstrong and Alvaro Mejia make last-minute decisions not to ride their Lotus bikes, so we prepare their spare time-trial bikes. This requires a quick switch of wheels, and some hasty calculations on how to mount Lotus bikes on a roof rack designed to carry standard frames. Talk about nerves!

Thankfully, the stage goes well for us — no mechanicals or crashes, and we come in sixth fastest of the 22 teams. Casartelli has a hard time hanging on after 10km, but manages to hold his place, unlike Ozers who is dropped at 20km and doesn't make the time limit. Armstrong, Peron and Yates are super-strong. After dismounting all the time-trial equipment and storing it away, we stand back, amazed at how much equipment is needed for a time trial. After fixing the road bikes for stage four, our day finally ends at 8:30 p.m.

Stage 3: Mayenne—Alençon TTT, 67km.

1. GEWISS-BALLAN (I); 2. ONCE (SP); 3. BANESTO (SP).

Overall: 1. JALABERT; 2. IVAN GOTTI (I), GEWISS-BALLAN; 3. BJARNE RIIS (DK), GEWISS-BALLAN.

July 5 Today is a pretty hilly stage. Yates hits a rock on a steep descent at 70 kph and his front tire blows out. If it were anyone but Yates, it probably would be an ugly crash. One of the worst things that can happen mechanically with a bike is to lose control in the front end after a fork or stem breaks or, in Yates's case, when a front tire punctures. There is nothing you can do about it, and it usually happens so fast.

There are a lot of bad crashes today. Hendrik Redant crashes badly in the neutralized area, and there is a crash two kilometers from the finish involving Laurent Jalabert, which costs him 48 seconds and the yellow jersey. The race has been unusually hard for mechanics so far, even though the race is looking good for us at Motorola. At dinner, Frankie Andreu asks us to put on 11-tooth cogs for stage five. He says they were spinning out in their 12s on today's finish! It's hard to believe how much faster cycling seems to get every year. Where does it end? The question stays with me until I finish working at 8 p.m.

Stage 4: Alençon—Le Havre, 162km

1. Cipollini; 2. Erik Zabel (G), Telekom; 3. Frédéric Moncassin (F), Novell.

Overall: 1. Gotti; 2. Riis; 3. Melchor Mauri (Sp), ONCE.

July 6 I wake up at 6 a.m., earlier than usual, to allow me enough time to change all the sprockets. General Chuck Boyd, a four-star Air Force General and Deputy Commander-in-Chief of the U.S. European Command, arrives with his whole security team to say hello to everyone on the team! A big cycling fan, he came to visit the race for a day in 1993 — the stage Lance won at Verdun. It's great having the general in our team car — he is a real pleasure to talk to.

The stage is pretty uneventful until eight kilometers from the finish, when there is a big crash involving Lance. Fortunately, I spot Lance standing up before I jump out, and see that he needs a new bike. Grabbing his bike from the roof rack, I run up to him, weaving my way between cars and other mechanics. Then, after getting him on his bike and on his way, we are called again on the race radio. Yates has wrecked a front wheel. When he looked behind for Lance, he accidentally let his front wheel spin into another rider's pedals. Again, it's hard to believe that he didn't crash.

Back at the hotel, I completely rebuilt Lance's bike; every part was destroyed. We finish work at 9 p.m., go to a Motorola social function at 10, and don't get into bed until 1:30 a.m. It will be pay-back time in five hours' time....

Stage 5: Fécamp—Dunkirk, 261km 1. Jerome Blijlevens (NL) TVM; 2. Jan Svorada (Slo) Lampre-Panaria; 3. Zabel.

Overall: 1. Gotti; 2. Riis; 3. Mauri.

July 7 As expected, it's a tall order this morning to wake up at 6:30, but then I'm not alone. While washing the cars, one of the soigneurs freaks out and starts throwing coolers around, apparently because we are wetting their work area. I hadn't even realized it. Then again, I'm still half-asleep. Nice way to start the day....

There's a huge crowd in Belgium. It's incredible how the biggest crowds in the Tour are so often outside France. I'm in a bad mood working on the bikes in the afternoon. The other mechanics are working pretty slowly and I start getting a little impatient because I just want to get all the work done and enjoy a good night's sleep. Sometimes, people just want to take their time working. But everybody has bad days on the Tour. You just have to get through them. I deliberately miss dinner, have a snack in the room, and go to bed early.

Stage 6: Dunkirk—Charleroi, 202km

1. Zabel; 2. Jalabert; 3. Abdujaparov.

Overall: 1. Riis; 2. Gotti; 3. Jalabert.

July 8 This looks likely to be a very exciting day, one we have all been waiting for. It's probably the stage that Lance has the best chance of winning in the whole Tour. Indeed, he makes it into a couple of small breaks toward the end. He is in a break with two others, when defending Tour champion Miguel Indurain bridges up like a rocket and

shells him as if he were standing still. I think it's a big surprise for
Lance to see someone so much stronger than him.

We are all pretty disappointed. Maybe Lance isn't in as good a shape
as everyone thought? It's a bad sign for the upcoming stages. You only
get so many chances, and this was a big one. Everyone hopes that
Lance's blunt edge is due to his continuing recovery from the injuries
he sustained in the crash at Dunkirk. Holding onto those hopes after
the stage, we put away the road bikes and mount the time-trial bikes
for tomorrow.

Stage 7: Charleroi—Liège, 203km

1. Johan Bruyneel (B), ONCE; 2. Miguel Indurain (Sp), Banesto; 3. Jesper Skibby (Dk), TVM.

Overall: 1. Bruyneel; 2. Indurain; 3. Jalabert.

July 9 Today is a big turning point for our hopes of a top overall placing. Everyone is hoping that Alvaro Mejia will do something in the
time trial — but he has a terrible ride. Maybe he will still have a good
day in the mountains....

Lance rides pretty well. Following him in the team car with Jim
Ochowicz and Eddy Merckx, we talk a lot about positioning and
Lance's position in particular. Eddy thinks that Lance is too far forward on his time-trial bike, which I agree with. I have already talked
to Lance about this. Eddy thinks a rider's time-trial position shouldn't
vary too much from his regular road position (the saddle position, relative to the crankset, that is, not the upper body). Lance's time-trial
position is significantly different than that on his road bike.

After the stage, I can't seem to find my way back to the hotel, as all
the main roads are closed because of the race. I finally succeed, and
then help organize everything for our evacuation to the Alps, where the
race will continue the day after tomorrow. All the time-trial equipment
returns by truck to our headquarters here in Belgium. Finally on the
road, we stop at McDonald's for a quick "McFeast." Everyone on the
team likes going to McDonald's. I don't know why, maybe it's that lit-

tle taste of home that the Americans like once in a while. We stop in the city of Nancy for the night, a little more than halfway to our destination, and prepare to drive the rest of the way to the Alps tomorrow.

Now that we are heading into the mountains, and with the first 10 days having produced no significant results, the pressure on us has suddenly increased. Everyone is a little more nervous. We had always targeted the first few days of the Tour as our big chance to win a stage or take the leader's yellow jersey. Once those days have passed, there are fewer chances to win; certainly a lot fewer than in the mountains ahead. Things suddenly look bleak for us....

Stage 8: Huy—Seraing TT, 54km

1. INDURAIN; 2. RIIS; 3. TONY ROMINGER (SWIT), MAPEI-GB.

Overall: 1. INDURAIN; 2. RIIS; 3. EUGENI BERZIN (RUS), GEWISS-BALLAN.

July 10 Rest days like today are always looked forward to, even though eventually they may not be too restful. Most of the staff prefers to get on with the race. In any case, there is still work to do. After their flight down from Belgium, the riders have to train, so their bikes need to be washed and fitted with training wheels, pumps and spare tires.

We are staying in a nice hotel set in the foothills of the Alps, with good service and food. The change from the hustle and bustle of the big cities to the beauty and serenity of the Alps is welcomed. This is the part of the Tour I really love. It's so relaxing in the mountains, at least when work is done. A walk or hike after work can provide that little bit of needed rejuvenation.

The race is always so different in the mountains, as well. Following in the team car down radical descents, holding on by the seat of your pants, can be very exciting. The stakes are always a lot higher in the mountains. The chance of riders or team cars crashing is much higher and, at the speeds experienced on mountain descents, that can be disastrous. Going downhill at perhaps 100 kph — with other team cars, press and police motorcycles just a few feet away and on both sides, and delayed riders trying to get back into the peloton — can make for a very nerve-racking time.

One year in the Alps, Sean Yates tried to bridge up to the first group from the second on a steep descent. The race officials allowed our team car to pass the chase group on a small uphill section before the descent continued, so we managed to get behind Sean and follow him down. Yates was then probably the best descender in pro cycling, and it was a joy to watch him go down this high-speed descent of long sweeping turns requiring little braking. As we came to one turn, I saw a rider who had flatted from the front group getting pushed off by his mechanic after a wheel change. Yates was catching him quickly and was right on his tail, just before they disappeared from view around the next turn.

As we entered the turn we realized we were going far too fast for that corner. It was an unusually sharp switchback, which was not consistent with the long and gentle curves of the descent so far. We held our breath ... and fortunately pulled through. Then I looked up in horror to see a rider lying in the rocks, wearing what I thought was a red jersey, next to a mangled bike that was sticking up into the air. I thought it was Sean — who had been going much faster into the turn than the other rider. Then, as we slowed, I took a better look and saw that it wasn't Sean. It was the rider who had flatted ... and the red on his jersey was blood.

On the outside of the turn, there was a large rock wall with boulders at the foot of it. He had ridden straight into it at full speed. It was a pretty grizzly sight.... I don't know how Sean had managed to stay upright, considering that he had been going even faster than the crashed rider.

July 11 The first big day in the mountains, and you can feel the excitement in the air. Today's stage is made up of six climbs, including two category one climbs and one *hors categorie* (or above-category) climb to the finish at the ski station summit of La Plagne. Stages don't get much tougher than this one.

It's a crazy start. We have put new titanium freewheel cassettes on the riders' bikes and, after they ride to the start, they all complain that their gears are grinding in one gear. So we have to execute a mad change of all their cassettes at the start. Unfortunately, some of the spare wheels had the new titanium cogs, so we don't have enough of the regular Shimano sprockets to go around. But we managed to fix everything in time.

Early in the stage, Alex Zülle from the ONCE team attacks with a couple of other riders … until he really puts the hammer down on the second category-one climb, the Cormet de Roseland.

Lance tries to bridge up to the leaders on the descent before the Roseland, but doesn't quite make it. Race leader Indurain's group isn't gaining much ground, and at the bottom of the last climb is four minutes down on Zülle — who goes on to a spectacular stage victory. Meanwhile, Indurain puts on the pressure, systematically drops everyone with him and closes to within two minutes of Zülle at the finish.

It suddenly starts hailing at the summit, the wind picks up, and by the time everyone has finished, the wind is so strong that it looks like some of the team trucks might blow over. It is next to impossible for us to work on the bikes, so we just give them a quick wash, stash them in the truck and decide to check everything tomorrow morning. Soaked to the bone, I stand in a hot shower for almost an hour before finally warming up.

Stage 9: Le Grand Bornand—La Plagne, 160km

1. ALEX ZÜLLE (SWIT),ONCE; 2. INDURAIN; 3. PAVEL TONKOV (RUS), LAMPRE-PANARIA.

Overall: 1. INDURAIN; 2. ZÜLLE; 3. RIIS.

July 12 Next to the final stage on the Champs-Elysées in Paris, L'Alpe d'Huez is probably the most famous and prestigious stage finish in the

Tour. We discovered *how* great an impact winning this stage has after Andy Hampsten took it in 1992, when he was with Motorola. Seeing pictures of him winning that stage brings back every emotional second of his winning climb to the top and the celebration afterward.

It's still dark and very cold when we start work today at 6:15 a.m. We wash all the cars and mount all the bikes from the day before. George leaves in the truck, and we drive the team cars in search of gas. Once again, we play "musical bikes" on the cars as the riders decide whether to ride down to the start at Aime-La Plagne. Most riders get carsick descending mountains in cars, so riding down is usually the final solution.

Halfway into the stage, a break of 11 riders escapes — without any Motorola riders. Thankfully, Mejia bridges across to join it. At the bottom of L'Alpe d'Huez, the break has 50 seconds on the main group which includes Indurain. The Italian climber Marco Pantani attacks and Indurain tries to go with him, but can't. Pantani and those who do go with him catch the break, whereupon Mejia is dropped. In his typically spectacular way, Pantani wins.

Except for Mejia in front, all our riders are split up into five or six groups, so we spend most of the day going back and forth between each group, handing up bottles and food. That's the normal duty of those in the second car. The first car always stays with the team's leading rider. However, after moving up and down the split-up field, we end up following Lance on today's final climb.

The 21-turn mountain road leading to L'Alpe d'Huez on Tour day is the most ridiculous mobfest I've ever seen, with the crowds 10- to 20-deep in places. People completely flood the road and only back out of the way as the riders pass. It's incredible to see; and you're not even sure where the road is going. You just ride toward a phalanx of people and hope that *you* don't drive off the side of the road. Most people have been on the mountainside since the night before and many have been on a drinking binge ever since. It's one big party with fans from all over Europe, and by the time the riders arrive a lot of the spectators are smashed. They tend to get a little "brave" and take risks in getting close to the riders. That's when accidents can happen.

As we get higher up the mountain, the crowd gets bigger, more out of control and less willing to part when Lance comes through. We hit numerous people with the car's rear-view mirrors and even run over a number of spectators' feet. I become nervous; the crowd seems so much more frenzied than ever before.

In a split second, Lance is down on the ground and the crowd is around him. Someone stuck his camera out in Lance's path to get a shot, pulled it back, but unwittingly allowed his strap to become caught around Lance's handlebars, taking Lance down. I push my way out the car door and fight through the crowd to Lance. A spectator has grabbed his bike and is reluctant to let go of it. I push people out of the way who are in between Lance and me, slip his chain back on and eventually push him off, as the crowd cheers. They love it, we don't!

Thankfully, for the last couple of kilometers the crowds are kept back by barriers … but it's not enough. The barriers need to be most of the way up. It's just too dangerous as it is. (When Hampsten won in '92, he had to push some people out of the way who were getting too close. Someone even tried to take his water bottle as he rode by. Five-time Tour winner Bernard Hinault, who was in the officials' car behind Andy, was kept busy using a stick to knock people out of the way.)

Geoff Brown, one of our mechanics in the other car, tells me later that he accidentally handed up the wrong bottle to Och when he asked for a water bottle to spray over Mejia. Not knowing he gave Och a bottle with a carbo drink instead, Mejia was suddenly covered in a sticky sweet liquid. In that heat, it must have been brutal. It all happens on the Tour … good and bad, funny and tragic.

Stage 10: Aime-La Plagne—L'Alpe d'Huez, 162.5km

1. Marco Pantani (I), Carrera; 2. Indurain; 3. Zülle.

Overall: 1. Indurain; 2. Zülle; 3. Riis.

July 13 A very hard race. The stage to St. Etienne is always a hard one. In a temperature of 35 degrees Celsius (over 100 degrees F), the riders really suffer. I am constantly filling bottles in the back seat. After the stage, the "Breaking Away" tour group from the U.S. shows up and Frankie Andreu and Sean Yates participate in a question-and-answer session with them. Afterward, they came over to the truck to watch us work and ask a bunch of questions. It's pleasant to have them around, a nice change of pace — not to mention the fact that it feels good to hear people speaking English for a change! It's a breath of fresh air having enthusiastic people around at this point in the Tour.

Stage 11: Bourg d'Oisans—St. Etienne, 199km

1. Max Sciandri (I), MG-Technogym; 2. Hernan Buenahora (Col), Kelme; 3. Rolf Aldag (G), Telekom.

Overall: No change.

July 14 Rusty Brasclear, the corporate vice-president for communications at Motorola who has spent the last few days with the team and with his son, Andy, start their last day with us. I don't think Rusty has been too impressed with our performance, though. Today, Peron gets into a break with five other riders, three of them from ONCE. Hennie tells him not to work, but he does anyway and finishes last out of the break. Jim is really pissed off at the finish. He can't believe that Peron would work in a break that contained three ONCE riders, especially after he was told not to. Neither can I....

Stage 12: St. Etienne—Mende, 222.5km

1. Jalabert; 2. Massimo Podenzana (I), BresciaLat; 3. Davide Bottaro (I), Gewiss-Ballan.

Overall: 1. Indurain; 2. Zülle; 3. Jalabert.

July 15 The soigneurs are getting a little grumpy. It's about that time! In a big tour, there is always a point when soigneurs decide that mechanics are the enemy and start treating us like we have the plague. It never fails. It's comical, and not worth letting it bother you.

It's a hard race today ... but they all are by this point in the Tour.

Lots of ups and downs on this 13th stage, both geographically and psychologically, as we are soon to discover. Lance is in a break with three others and they stay away for more than 200km. On the last climb, the St. Ferréol hill at Revel, Lance and Sergei Uchakov — a Ukrainian on the Polti team — drop the other two. We think that Lance has it in the bag … a stage win, finally. But then Lance is beaten in the sprint! Uchakov leads it out and makes the sprint a very short one, not giving Lance the time to come around him. What a day … an opportunity that is so hard to come by suddenly slips away.

We go to our hotel straight after the finish. The soigneurs drive very dangerously, taking too many risks. Too many for me anyhow. I ask them to slow down, saying there's no rush; but they just get pissed off. I should have known. Yates drops out today as well. Yup, a bad day….

Stage 15: Mende-Revel, 245km

1. Sergei Uchakov (Ukr), Polti; 2. Lance Armstrong (USA), Motorola; 3. Bruno Cenghialta (I), Gewiss-Ballan.

Overall: No change.

July 16   Get up early this morning. The weather report says there is a very small chance of showers, so we don't put on the rain tires. Five times since the Tour started we have changed everyone's wheels at the last minute, because of the forecast of rain, and not once did it rain. This time, we decide to blow it off, and what happens? It pours!

Such fate reflects our blessings … or lack of them. Mejia is dropped early on the first big climb, the second-category Port de Lers at 129km. It isn't a good sign, considering he's our No. 1 climber. It pretty much seals his fate for a contract in 1996. You only get so many chances, and the Colombian has had more than he should have. There are a couple of really dangerous descents, lots of crashes and, because of the rain, it is a pretty nervous race. Our chances for a stage victory are quickly vanishing, and the pressure on the team is mounting.

Some riders are complaining about having sore butts — it's no wonder in such a long race! We change the saddle on Swart's bike…. We also borrow a big fat cyclo-tourist saddle from another team for Frankie. Tour riders are so skinny, they've got no meat on their butt.

Pantani wins on his own again. He's the best pure climber I've ever seen. No one can ride with him in the mountains when he is at his best.

Stage 14: St. Orens-de-Gameville—Guzet-Neige, 164km

1. PANTANI; 2. LAURENT MADOUAS (F), CASTORAMA; 3. INDURAIN.

Overall: NO CHANGE.

July 18 Today starts out normally: We wash the team cars, get the bikes ready, load the cars, do everything we usually do before a stage. Little do we know that today will be a day that no one will ever forget.

I really can't remember in detail any of the events before we get *the call* over the race radio. I remember distinctly the moment we hear the French words: "*Chute, chute*" ("Crash, crash") on Radio Tour, as we are descending the Col de Portet d'Aspet. The voice seems to have more urgency in it than normal. I get an uneasy feeling waiting for the car to slow, and listen as they give the names of the teams in the crash. They don't call Motorola, and normally I would hesitate before jumping out; but I have an uneasy feeling about this one.

I leap out of the car and run down the hill. One of the first to arrive, I scan the scene quickly to see if there are any of our riders involved, but at first I don't see anybody. As I get closer, I spot the scene that is now imbedded in my memory forever. The race doctor, Gérard Porte, looks up at me as he holds Fabio Casartelli's head in his hands. Fabio is lying in the fetal position, and a pool of blood has already spread down the hill. I can't believe how much blood there is. His bike lies in a heap beside him. I just stand there and stare; it can't have been for very long, but everything seems to move so slowly. The doctor is yelling, but I don't hear. I can't take my eyes off Fabio.

Finally, I am jolted out of my trance by a deafening scream. Reality comes rushing back to me when a race official next to me has his foot

run over by a car trying to squeeze by the accident site. The race has
gone mad, people are yelling and car horns are honking. It all seems
so surreal.

I have never hesitated before. A mechanic's priority is always to
make sure that the bike is okay if the rider wants to continue, but I
just stand there in a daze. As I look down at Fabio, the blood continues to spread down the road. I know he isn't going to make it. Finally,
I decide to get his bike off the road. The saddle is pushed up against
the small of his back, and for some reason I am afraid to pull it away;
as if I might disturb him.

I pull the bike away slowly and Fabio's body moves slightly. As I
pick up the bike, I look into the doctor's eyes for some sign of hope;
but there is none. I walk back to the car, carrying the bike, and Jim
Ochowicz is just walking up. Stopping him, I say, "It doesn't look
good, Jim, he's in very bad shape."

Jim goes to see for himself, while I put the bike on the roof. When
he returns, his face is white with shock. We stand there for a few
moments; he is in a daze. I finally ask him, "What do you want to do?
We can either stay, or we can have Hennie stay with him. One of us
needs to get back in the race." Jim ponders for a few moments and
says, "We should probably go. Hennie can wait with him."

We don't say much while trying to rejoin the race. The gravity of
the situation is beginning to sink in. Radio Tour informs us that a
helicopter is on its way to take Fabio to the hospital. A few minutes
later, Hennie confirms that this has occurred and that he is back on
the road again.

"How is he, Hennie? Did the doctor tell you anything?" asks Jim.

"It's very bad, Jim. He hit his head very hard," answers Hennie to Jim,
who looks at me in the mirror and says, in disbelief: "He could die."

After all the years Jim has been in cycling, he never imagined that
something like this could really happen. We don't talk very much over
the next few hours, overcome by the realization that we may have lost

a teammate and friend. Radio Tour gives periodic updates, and finally the news of Fabio's death arrives. The sadness in the voice on the radio is clear. We hope it will be good news, even though deep down we know it won't be.

Neither Jim nor I is fluent in French, but we understand what is being said on the radio. "What did he say?" asks Jim to our French guest, who had been respectfully quiet during the whole ordeal.

"It's over," he says quietly.

"He died?" I ask, hoping that I had misunderstood or that I was experiencing a nightmare and would soon awake.

"Yes," he answers solemnly.

It's quiet for a long time as the magnitude of our friend's death sinks in. You can feel the grief in the air. It isn't only our team that is affected, but the entire race … every person, from officials to sponsors, press and fans. They all feel the loss.

By the time we get to the finish line, someone has given the news to all of the riders in the peloton, and the press is swarming around our team car, trying to document the grief we all feel. The soigneurs try to keep them back, but it's impossible. I put the bikes on the roof and go about my work, trying not to be overwhelmed by my emotions. There are people crying everywhere it's hard to maintain control. Finally, Stephanie Adams from Oakley, who I have known for years, asks if I am okay and gives me a hug. I crack. The tears start coming and I can't stop them. I don't want to let her go. Finally, I manage to get control of myself and walk away, needing some fresh air and a few moments to myself. Getting myself together, I return to the team cars where everyone is staring at us. I keep my eyes lowered, not wanting to see the sadness in the others' eyes.

Finally, we get back to the hotel. Very little is said as we unload the cars. No one is really sure what to say. Hennie comes out and asks if we want to go to the hospital to see Fabio. We are all a little surprised and unsure what to do. I want to go and say to the other mechanics that we can do the bikes in the morning. We all go, and Massimo Testa, the Motorola team doctor, comes out to explain to us what happened to Fabio. He says that Fabio received a massive blow to the head that fractured his skull, and his heart stopped three times in the helicopter en route to the hospital. He underwent emergency surgery, but there was nothing that could be done. The blow was simply far too severe, and he passed away.

We go in the hospital and see Fabio lying there. He's unrecognizable, with a bandage around his head. Returning to the hotel, we have a meeting at which the riders decide to continue the Tour. It is what Fabio would have wanted; there is no point in quitting.

Stage 15: St. Girons—Cauterets, 206 km

1. Richard Virenque (F), Festina; 2. Claudio Chiappucci (I), Carrera; 3. Buenahora.

Overall: 1. Indurain; 2. Zülle; 3. Riis.

July 19 After little sleep, we get up early and prepare the bikes for the stage. Fabio's bike is placed in the No. 1 position on the roof rack in his honor. Jim wants it that way. So Fabio's bike, and in a way his spirit, will make it all the way to Paris.

At the start, a minute's silence is held in memory of Fabio. All you can hear are the hundreds of camera shutters clicking and flashes going off as the press gets its fill of grief on film. Amazingly, a fight actually breaks out between a couple of photographers trying to get the best shot. I can't believe it.

After starting the stage, it feels strange that life is continuing, or trying to anyhow. It's weird that after all that has happened, it's business as usual on the Tour. It is super hot today and there is practically no wind. On one climb, many riders are dropped, not because it's a fast race, but because the riders have decided not to attack today and just ride the stage at a very slow pace. Even so, riders are still wilting under the heat on this long, long stage through the Pyrenees, with a brewing sense of grief for Fabio's death. Johan Museeuw, who was in the crash with Fabio, can barely pedal and is dropped. Yesterday at the crash site, he was just sitting there staring at Fabio when I arrived. It must have really freaked him out.

Eventually, the stage becomes one of the longest in recent memory. The field arrives two hours after the estimated time of finish in Pau. Then, the peloton — having decided to donate all the prize money from the stage to a trust fund set up overnight for Fabio's family — lets our riders lead the Tour into Pau with two kilometers to go. After the finish, we are swarmed by the press again, and there are problems because no one from Motorola wants to go to the podium to accept the stage laurels. Although Peron is first across the line, the Tour organizers declare all the results void.

Stage 16: Tarbes—Pau, 237km

No stage results due to this being declared a neutralized stage.

July 20 Today is much better; people are starting to smile again and get back into their routine. But Fabio's death has given everyone a reality check and a new perspective on life. It makes you realize how some things you worry about are so trivial, like the ongoing battle the mechanics have with the soigneurs. A tragedy makes you realize what's really important in life and what isn't. It's nice to see moods changing for the better. Today is a typical sprinter's race, as the stage to Bordeaux always is. Just a few more days to go. I'm really looking forward to going home for a couple of days.

Stage 17: Pau—Bordeaux, 246km

1. Zabel; 2. Abdujaparov; 3. Stefano Colage (I), ZG-Telekom.

Overall: No change.

July 21 This is a pretty hard stage — and a very exciting one. There are lots of breaks on a tough course with rolling hills. The pressure for teams like us that haven't yet won a stage is intense.

I'm in the second car with Hennie when there is an escape by 12 riders, including Lance. Their lead grows to two minutes. Then Lance catches the break off guard by attacking with 28km to go, on a slight uphill. It's a perfect move. The others just sit and look at one another. A few guys try to bridge the gap on their own, but are caught. Then the chase slows down because they can't get organized.

Hennie and I go up in the team car and follow Lance. He's flying and seemingly feels no pain, so determined is he to win — as he does in brilliant style. Crossing the finish line, he raises his arms and looks to the sky as if to say: "This is for you, Fabio!" It's a very emotional moment for us all, one of many we've had over the last few days. It's also a very important day for us, and helps us to finish the Tour on a good note instead of a solely tragic chord.

Stage 18: Montpon-Ménestérol—Limoges, 166.5km

1. ARMSTRONG; 2. ANDREA FERRIGATO (I), ZG-TELEKOM; 3. VITACHESLAV EKIMOV (RUS), NOVELL.

Overall: NO CHANGE.

July 22 The weather is terrible — rainy, cold and miserable. I follow Lance in this final time trial. He goes pretty easy to avoid crashing. I have a meeting with a few of the riders tonight to discuss our technical program, and find out what they think of it, and where they think we can provide better support. It goes very well. I expect a big bitch session, but they are all very positive and constructive.

Stage 19: Lac de Vassivière TT, 46.5km

1. INDURAIN; 2. RIIS; 3. ROMINGER.

Overall: NO CHANGE.

July 23 This is my favorite stage, probably most people's favorite as well. It's incredible that after so many miles they still manage to go so fast. These guys have been put through the wringer and back, and they still have it in their legs to go hard. It's an incredible stage. The grandstands at the finish in Paris are filled to the hilt and the entire finishing circuit is jammed with up to 250,000 people.

As we enter the Champs-Elysées on the first of nine 6.5km laps, the crowd roars with excitement. On one of the circuits, just as we are passing the grandstands, Sean Yates flats and I jump out of the car. The adrenaline pumps through my veins as the deafening screams of the crowd continue. They love it. I pray that I won't blow it here, in front of thousands of people and international television. Fortunately, I don't, and I push Sean off without a hitch.

As we bring him back up through the team cars behind our car, I notice that he's spun out in his 12-cog gearing on the cobbles. We are flying along at 60 kph and barely gaining ground on the peloton. Finally, we get Frankie back in. Then Mejia gets in a small break — the last rider we expect to see on this stage; but that group is caught and sets the race up for a sprint finish. It goes to Djamolidin Abdujaparov, a nice result for him after he had finished second so many times.

After the race, we begin the big evacuation from Paris, clean up and return all the Fiats, and pack up the truck. The team goes out for the traditional dinner, and we all have a great time. It's a perfect finish to my last and arguably most traumatic Tour de France.

Stage 20: Ste. Geneviève-des-Bois—Paris (Champs-Elysées), 155km

1. ABDUJAPAROV; 2. GIANMATTEO FAGNINI (I), MERCATONE UNO-SAECO; 3. LOMBARDI.

Final result: 1. INDURAIN; 2. ZÜLLE; 3. RIIS; 4. JALABERT; 5. GOTTI.

chapter eight

the Pro
Bike Wash
and Preparation for Competition

After two years with the Coors Light team, I could never have imagined that my education as a professional mechanic was only just starting when I arrived at Motorola in Europe. But it is only in Europe where the true art of being a good team mechanic can be learned. I got through those first years at Coors Light because of my youth and enthusiasm, not to mention the fact that I was able to work with some of the best people in cycling, team manager Len Pettyjohn in particular. But when I got to Europe, I soon realized that I had a lot more to learn.

There are still no courses to take or books to read in which you can learn how to be a good team mechanic — not even this one. To be a good team mechanic is something you can only learn firsthand. When I started, I would almost always work with another mechanic and just follow his lead. The big drawback in that process is that no one ever sits down and explains what the heck is going on, or why you just did what you did. Learning comes by using your own initiative to take in everything you saw or heard. I wasted so much time and energy doing completely unnecessary things and being inefficient, simply because there was no direction or one-on-one instruction.

People often ask me what it's like being a mechanic, and whether the stories are true about mechanics staying up until 2 a.m. under a street lamp in some hotel parking lot overhauling bottom brackets for the next day's race. I hate to say it but, in many cases, these stories *are* true and I've experienced many of them myself — but only in the U.S. It happens that way because most U.S. teams and mechanics lack experience and suffer from acute disorganization. But U.S. racing has a forgiving schedule of races that allows you to ignore inadequacies that would destroy a team in Europe. If a mechanic was that disorganized in Europe, he would only last about a month with the intense racing schedule. It's no coincidence that many mechanics in Europe are more than 40 years old. Indeed, some are as old as 60 and have been team mechanics their entire professional lives. Do you think they would have lasted that long had they been up until 2 a.m. washing bikes every night? No way!

Master mechanics have refined the job into an art, and the foundation of that art is preparation and organization. Much of a mechanic's job focuses on the preparation needed long before a race ever happens. But just as important is how efficient and organized you are when you get there. With Coors Light, I wasted so much time checking things over and over again, sometimes even missing things that *did* need my attention. Europe, however, prompted a major change and, over the years, my own time-efficient and thorough pattern of preparing bicycles for competition evolved. Most people are not team mechanics and never will be. Nonetheless, the following procedures will come in handy for most cyclists at some point in their careers. Who knows, maybe a mechanic won't be on hand to check your gear before a race? And for those who are mechanics, this might help them refine their techniques and ultimately improve their work.

THE PRO BIKE WASH

Before you get started, make sure you have the following:

- Soap: dishwashing detergent is good, and Dawn is the best because it cuts grease well.
- Degreaser or diesel fuel.
- Frame sponge: large and soft enough to wrap completely around frame tubes.
- Drivetrain sponge.
- Drivetrain brush: pick a paint brush with stiff bristles.
- Handlebar brush: get a brush with soft bristles.
- Hub brush: try a bottle brush with reasonably stiff bristles.
- Spoke brush: dustpan type.
- Bucket: for soapy water.
- Hose, with water connected, or rinse bucket with clean water and sponge.
- Something to hold the chain in the dropouts - an old axle with quick release, or even a long screwdriver inserted through the cutouts in the rear dropouts.

Now, to carry out the pro wash, do the following:

- Put the bicycle in the bike stand, remove the wheels, install a chain device so chain doesn't rub on chainstay when cranks are turning.
- Apply liberal amount of degreaser to the chain while it's in the big chainring — where it passes over the chain device and above the rear derailleur while turning the cranks.
- Brush both sides of the chain with drivetrain brush while turning cranks, and paint both sides of the chainrings, derailleurs, pedal spindles, and upper and lower headsets while applying degreaser to the brush as needed.
- Apply degreaser to the rear-wheel cogset and scrub as necessary then rinse.
- Wrap the frame sponge around the tire and rim and go around the wheel a couple of times. Using the spoke brush, go around the wheel

at the rim and wash nipples on both sides. Then, wash spokes in an up-and-down motion around both sides of the entire wheel; wash the hub body with the hub brush, and wash the axle-dustcap area with the drivetrain sponge to remove any grease that has squirted out.

• Do the same with the front wheel and rinse both wheels.

• Load the drivetrain sponge with water, wrap it around the chain and squeeze as it enters the rear derailleur, while turning the cranks. Do this until the dripping water becomes clean.

• Wash the drivetrain with the drivetrain sponge, then wash the chainrings, derailleurs, pedal spindles and headset until degreaser is removed.

• With the frame sponge, wash the rest of the bike with lots of soapy water in this order: stem, handlebars, brake levers, cables, head tube, brake caliper, fork, top tube, down tube, saddle (top and underneath), seatpost, seat tube, seatstays, brake caliper, chainstays, dropouts and bottom of bottom-bracket shell.

• With the handlebar brush, scrub the handlebar tape with the grain of the tape — front to back, not side to side, otherwise it will rip.

• Rinse thoroughly, and leave to dry.

THE PRO INSPECTION

• Wipe the frame down with a clean soft rag to remove any excess water and water spots.

• Wipe the drivetrain down with a separate rag, to remove excess water from chain and water spots from components.

• Lubricate all pivot points and moving parts on the derailleurs, pulley wheels, brake calipers and levers, and wipe off excess.

• Carefully inspect the entire frame and fork for stress cracks and signs of frame failure. (Also inspect the saddle rails, seatpost cradle, and stem for the same problem signs.)

• Handlebars have a tendency of "drooping" over time, so measure the distance from center to center of the handlebar drops. If you have 42cm bars and they measure only 40.5cm, then you should consider changing them. (Note: some bars don't measure center to center).

- Check every nut and bolt on the bike and make sure nothing is loose. Start at one end of the bike and work your way to the other end. Remember, there is a fine line between "tight enough" and "too tight." You don't, for example, want to apply the same torque to your pulley wheel bolts as you do to your crank bolts.
- Inspect all cables and cable-housings for wear and cracking, and replace as necessary. Make sure all cable ends are capped.
- Inspect wheels:
  a) Inspect sidewalls on each side for cuts and rotting.
  b) Go around the tire and check the condition of the tread, and check all cuts for glass and debris. Remove any fragments and check to make sure the cut is not through the tread and into the casing — through the first layer of casing may be okay, but no more.
  c) If the tire is a sew-up, carefully inspect the entire circumference of the wheel to make certain that the tire is still glued on well. A recently mounted clincher should be deflated and inspected, to ensure that the tube is not somehow pinched between the bead and the rim.
  d) Turn the axle to make sure that it spins freely and smoothly, and does not feel gritty. Make sure that it has a small amount of play in it.
  e) Inspect the rim for cracking at the eyelets and to make sure that none of the spoke nipples are beginning to pull through.
  f) Check to make sure that the freehub retaining ring is tight and the cogs are not overly worn.
  g) Repeat procedure on the front wheel.
  h) Install the rear wheel correctly! Place the wheel in the dropouts, and grasp the rim and pull upward and back, while you close the skewer. This ensures that the axle is in the most rearward position and seated against the *tops* of the dropouts, *not* the bottoms. The

wheel must be installed this way because once the rider is on the bike and applying force to the pedals, the wheel will try to work its way back to that position if it isn't already there. If you change a wheel in a race, this is the natural position the wheel will take in the dropouts. If the wheel was not originally installed in this position, then the brakes and shifting may not be adjusted properly with the new wheel installed, even if the wheels are dished the same. It can be a real pain if the brakes are rubbing while the rider is trying to get back into the peloton. Despite this, there are a lot of mechanics who do not realize that this is the way a wheel has to be installed. In fact, some European pro mechanics take the bike out of the stand and install the rear wheel on the ground to ensure its proper positioning.

i) Make sure that the wheel is straight in the frame between the chainstays, and also straight relative to the seatstays. If you have a problem lining up the wheel in the seatstays and chainstays at the same time, remove the wheel and check the dish. If it is okay, take some time to check the alignment of the frame.

j) While holding your thumb against one of the brake pads, spin the wheel and check for "trueness" and roundness. True the wheel if necessary. This may require you to remove the wheel and true it in a stand. Squeeze each set of spokes to check for any loose spokes or uneven tension.

k) Grasp the rim and wiggle side to side, to check for any play in the hub. If it is loose, remove and adjust. Spin the wheel to make sure it spins freely, and hold the seatstay to check for vibration from a gritty hub. If necessary, overhaul the hub.

• Squeeze the brake lever and make sure that the cable is running smoothly and easily. Center the brakes. Check brake-pad wear and position, replace and adjust as necessary. Check for play in the brake caliper and adjust as necessary. Adjust the brake barrel adjuster, to loosen or tighten if necessary. Remember, every rider likes his brakes fine-tuned differently, so try to remember each rider's individual preferences.

- Remove the chain from the chainring. Hold onto the seat tube a few inches above the bottom bracket and spin the cranks. Listen and feel for vibration from grit in the bearings. Check for play in the crankarms and adjust, or overhaul, as necessary.
- Put the chain back on the chainring and shift onto the outer cog. While turning the crank with your hand, shift the derailleur up onto the biggest cog and make sure it doesn't go into the spokes or past the last cog; release and make sure it goes back out to the smallest cog cleanly, and not past, into the frame. Do this a few times and adjust limit screws as necessary.
- Check the chain for excessive wear and replace if necessary.
- Check shifting. Go through the gears in both chainrings, trying to "throw" the chain, and adjust as necessary. Then do the same on the front, trying to throw the chain off the small and big chainring, while in a number of combinations on the back. Make sure shifting is crisp and clean and that the cables are running smoothly.
- Twist the handlebars from side to side and make sure that the headset moves freely and is not gritty.
- Install the front wheel. Inspect the hub. Check for trueness and roundness and make certain that the wheel sits in the fork straight. Check and adjust the brake just like you did on the rear.
- Remove and replace handlebar tape if necessary.
- Make sure the computer is functioning properly.
- Lubricate the chain.
- Remove the bicycle from the stand. Loosen the headset until it rattles when you bounce it and then slowly tighten it until the rattling is gone.
- Bounce the bike and listen for any unusual sounds or rattles. At this point, a broken frame will often make its presence known if you missed it before.

- Make sure the handlebars, saddle and brake levers are tight, and that the saddle and bars are straight. Do not straighten if slightly off, but check with the rider the next day. His idea of straight and yours may differ. I had devised a perfect method to determine if a stem was straight. But, even after double- and triple-checking it, some riders insisted that their bars were still crooked. I finally had to conclude that many stems are not machined at a perfect 90-degree angle to the bars. So, while the stem might be perfectly straight, the bars sit in them slightly crooked. This problem is quite common, so don't be too surprised if you encounter it.

All of these things don't need to be done every day. In the big tours, each mechanic works on the same bike throughout the entire race, so he knows which procedure has been recently carried out and which has not. Keeping the same mechanic on a bike throughout a major stage race makes sense, since he will be more familiar with that bicycle and its recent maintenance history. A mechanic may, for example, choose not to check bolts every day, but rather just a couple of times a week. If we were to switch bike assignments every day, many of those procedures would have to be carried out every day as well.

Wheels and tires, however, must be checked all the time. Frames should also be inspected regularly for cracks. Of course, you also need to make sure the brakes and shifting systems are working properly. If a rider has crashed his bike, it's very important to take extra time to inspect the frame and its alignment. Be sure to straighten all parts like the handlebars and the seat, and check the rear derailleur alignment if it looks like the bike took a hit. This is not a time to cut corners. If there is a question about a part, replace it. Saving a couple of bucks is not worth the risk of failure.

THE PRO TOOLBOX

All these items are not absolutely necessary, but by having this stuff in the toolbox, a mechanic's job is made a heck of a lot easier.

• A good tool box with a lock, ideally palette style, with holders for your most frequently used tools and a spot for the biggest tools in the lower compartment.

• Allen wrenches:

    a) A folding multi-wrench tool with a full range of metric sizes

    b) L-shaped Allen wrenches in 4mm, 5mm and 6mm sizes. These are ideal for high torque items like stem bolts.

    c) Screwdriver-style Allen wrenches in 4mm, 5mm and 6mm sizes. These are perfect for hard-to-reach spots like seatpost-cradle bolts, bottle-cage bolts and time-trial-bar problems.

    d) T-handled Allen wrenches in 4mm, 5mm and 6mm sizes. These are great for everything, like seat binder bolts!

• Screwdrivers:

    a) Flathead: small one for computer mount, medium one for everything, and a large one for shoe cleats and high-torque items.

    b) Phillips: a small and medium one will suffice.

• Channel locks, regular pliers, needlenose pliers and cutters.

• Tire levers.

• Cone wrenches: a variety, to cover numerous sizes.

• Cable cutters.

• Box knife or razor-blade knife.

• A reamer: nice for making holes in plastic frame numbers.

• Chain-wear tool: measures chain stretch.

• Chainring bolt tool: for holding the backs of chainring bolts.

• Two chain tools and spare pins: you never know when you might need them!

• A medium and large crescent wrench.

• Crank puller: Campagnolo is the only way to go here!

• A 15mm open-end wrench: for crank puller.

• Tap handles with an assortment of taps: at least a couple of 5mms

• Tape measure.

- Vernier calipers: not necessary, but nice to know you have them.
- Ball peen hammer and rubber mallet.
- Pedal wrench.
- Headset wrenches.
- Various bottom-bracket installation tools.
- Two chain whips.
- Assortment of files: at least one flat file and one rat-tail file.
- Foldable wheel-dishing tool.
- Fourth-hand tool.
- Cogset lockring tool and/or various freewheel tools.
- A 14mm crankarm wrench.
- H-tools: for checking dropout alignment.
- Derailleur hanger alignment tool: Shimano is the brand to get.
- Pipe cutter: a must for trimming handlebars.
- Electrical tape.
- Disc adapter for pump.
- A pick: for inspecting cuts in tires.
- Hole punch.
- Scissors.
- Grease and chain lubricant.
- Gapping tools: for gapping spare wheels, preferably same type as your team bikes.
- Work apron.
- Black marker and a pen.

And last, but not least:
- A bottle opener: after a long day's work, you'll be looking for this one!

chapter nine

Life after the Tour

A lthough the Tour de France is the pinnacle of the season, there are many important races afterward — including the final World Cup events, the world championships and Tour of Spain (Vuelta a España). Riders who missed the cut for a place on a Tour team are usually pretty anxious to be racing again. For some, it may have been four weeks since they last raced and that really takes its toll on form, particularly compared with those riders who *did* race the Tour and are usually in great shape. It's also a nervous time for riders who haven't yet secured contracts for the following year and are desperate to impress the team directors before time runs out!

After a couple of days in Belgium of R&R after the Tour, I'd usually go to Spain for one of my favorite events of the year: the Tour of Burgos. Burgos is a good size city in the desert, about two-and-a-half hour's drive southwest of San Sebastian.

Spain has always been my favorite country. Besides the great weather and food, I always found the people to be very friendly. I also love the laid-back mentality of the Spaniards. If there is one thing I learned from living in Europe — particularly in Spain — it's to take time for the important things in life, like friends and family, and enjoy a good meal with them. North Americans get so caught up in the business side of life, they often lose perspective of what's truly important.

Spain was also a welcome change after the craziness of the Tour de France, as the Tour of Burgos is a very relaxed event. We stayed in the same hotel from start to finish, and since the mechanic who missed the Tour usually did it with me, he would follow the race in the team car every day while I did the hotel run. After five days of good food, sun and hanging out at the municipal pool, I was refreshed and ready to tackle the rest of the season. The Tour of Burgos is the best kept secret around. Surprisingly, no one from the staff wanted to do it ... except me!

Once we hired a part-time Belgian soigneur named François, who we had never used before. He was a nice guy, but didn't speak a word of English. At Burgos, he drove the second team car (probably for the show, two team cars were nearly always allowed to follow the race in Spain, even on flat stages). One day François, who had little experience of driving in a race caravan, hit a motorcycle cop from behind, putting him in the hospital. It was a really bad scene and marked the end of François's career with the Motorola team. Not surprising really....

After the Tour of Burgos, we moved on to San Sebastian in the Basque Country for the Clasica San Sebastian, a very hard and hilly World Cup race. The 1992 edition marked Lance Armstrong's debut in the European peloton, as he turned pro right after the Olympics in Barcelona. That year, the San Sebastian race experienced terrible weather, more like the classics in April: cold, wet and very windy.

Lance wasn't feeling very good in the race and told Hennie Kuiper that he wasn't sure why. Lance normally never suffered on climbs like these. But a lot of riders were dropped, and this prompted Lance to ask Hennie what he should do. Without hesitation, Hennie told him to try to make it to the finish. Lance's face as he looked at Hennie mirrored his surprise. "You want me to try and finish?" asked Lance, bewildered as much as he was exhausted.

The weather was getting even worse. Looking out the car window was like watching a television news report of a tornado: the palm trees were bent over, unbelievably refusing to break, and spectators were leaning into the wind to avoid being blown over!

Lance was dropped as soon as the race became hard, and I knew that was the last time we would see him for the day. When we arrived at the finish, very few riders were left in the race; most of our guys had abandoned. I layered up with as many raincoats as I could, put the bike of the one Motorola rider who did finish, Max Sciandri, on the race car and radioed to Hennie that I was done.

"Are you ready to go?" I asked Hennie, who was having a coffee in a little café near the team cars.

"We should wait for Lance," he said.

"What? You think he might still be riding out there?" I answered, totally shocked at the thought that Lance was still riding on his own … out there in this "hurricane."

"Well the broom wagon hasn't come in yet, so someone is still out there," answered Hennie.

I hadn't even noticed that the broom wagon wasn't in. So we waited for what seemed like forever, while I started thinking about how much work there was to do back at the hotel. Then, while looking into the distance — mesmerized by the bending wind-blown palm trees — I noticed a few cars and what looked like a bike rider approaching. It was Lance. I couldn't believe it; he had actually kept going this entire time, while others dropped out around him like flies. Not only was he the last to finish, but he was the last by 27 minutes. I was so sure he wasn't still racing that I hadn't even left a spot on the car for his bike, and the soigneurs had left long ago. Suddenly, I was scrambling in the driving rain to figure out where to put his bike.

If I had have known Lance better at that time, I wouldn't have been as surprised. He's the kind of person who, if he says he's going to do something, he does it. Three years later, in 1995, Lance won the

Clasica San Sebastian in spectacular fashion, attacking on the descent of the Jaizkibel mountain and riding away to record the first-ever World Cup race victory by a U.S. rider. The win was doubly importantly for Lance because of his poignant memories of this race. From a distant last to a spectacular first was quite an achievement.

The few days after the Clasica were nightmares for the mechanics, because there were usually 13 or 14 riders from the team on hand, all of them coming and going. The day after the Clasica, there is a one-day race in Urkiola, a big climbers' race that Andy Hampsten won twice in his career. Then, the day after Urkiola, comes the start of the Tour of Galicia — a region of Spain just north of Portugal. It was an organizational challenge for every mechanic.

Galicia is a very beautiful region, not dry and arid like Burgos and so many other parts of Spain. Galicia is lush with vegetation, right on the Atlantic Ocean and famous for seafood. The race was often rewarding for the team, as well. In 1992, Lance won a stage there — his first win as a pro — just after his nightmare in San Sebastian; and in 1993, Hampsten was first overall.

The only downside to the race was that the area is so remote. From San Sebastian, it's a full day's drive on small two-lane roads … and an even longer drive awaited us after it was over. Usually on the last day, I would leave in the team truck with one of the soigneurs before the stage start and set out on the marathon drive to the start of the Tour of the Netherlands. That race may have been closer to our home base, but it has never been my favorite. The Dutch terrain is so flat; after the sun and excitement of Spain, it was always a dull event for me.

After the 1995 Dutch Tour, we headed back to Spain for the three-week Vuelta a España. That was my first Vuelta, and I found it most enjoyable; nothing like the Tour de France, but similar to the Giro d'Italia in many ways — relatively poor organization, some pretty dubious hotels … but a lot of character and fun.

During a stage in the final week of that year's Vuelta, half of the peloton stopped on the roadside after an hour's racing for what most thought was a pee. Yet within 30 minutes, most riders were found pants down and suffering from diarrhea — including the ONCE team race leader Laurent Jalabert. Those teams all stayed at the same hotel the night before and ate the same — obviously contaminated — food.

A couple of directeurs sportifs from teams not affected by the problem wanted to take advantage of the situation, and asked Jim Ochowicz to help them make a big attack to blow the race apart. Fortunately, Jim decided against doing what was akin to kicking someone while he was down. Such an idea is so unsportsmanlike and only gives you a bad reputation. Although, it's surprising how often things like that do happen. Some teams will do anything to win.

A couple of days after that incident, on stage 19 into Calatayud, the bunch came hurtling down the finishing straight for a mass sprint. Motorola rider George Hincapie was in the front, in good position, when Marcel Wüst, a German from the Castelblanc team, tried to sprint through a gap where there wasn't one and took George down from behind. George didn't even see it coming and went head first into the barriers. Later, at dinner, he walked in wearing a large neck brace. My first reaction was of relief; it was good to see him walking again so soon after the crash. As for Wüst, he was lucky to escape punishment from a certain Motorola mechanic…. Watching the replay on television ` that night, I was so pissed. Wüst was totally out of line and could have killed someone. Having just been through the death of Fabio, it affected me more than it would have otherwise. Overall, the 1995 Vuelta produced a pleasant change of pace, as it was the first time the race had been held in September, having traditionally held an April-May slot.

Normally, my September schedule began with the Giro del Veneto in Italy, followed by the Grand Prix de Formies in France, and then Paris-Brussels and the Grand Prix Impanis in Belgium. The series would continue with the Grand Prix d'Isbergues in France, and three one-day races in Italy called the Trittico Premondiale, which were used by the Italians as selection events for world's. Even though there were fewer days of racing in this schedule than in the Vuelta, it was still more hectic for mechanics and team personnel because of all the traveling around Europe and the time stuck in limbo between races.

In the last 15km of the Grand Prix d'Isbergues in 1992, Phil Anderson was in a three-man breakaway when he had a rear-wheel change from neutral service before our team car could join the break. Upon reaching him, we saw Phil had been given a seven-speed freewheel, and not an eight speed one, making it impossible for his gears to work properly. Phil was really freaked out. He felt good and believed he could win, were it not for his slipping gears. He yelled at me: "Scott, I can't finish the race with this wheel. I need a wheel change!"

"Okay...." I replied, my answer cut short by Phil, who added, "Yup ... but you don't understand; it's gotta be fast!"

I didn't think about it then, but it makes me nervous to think about it today. We pulled over and I gave him one of the fastest wheel changes of my career. I don't think your technique ever changes. Fate probably influences the outcome, as much as a cool head does. That day, I was lucky, and Phil rejoined the break and went on to win. It was fantastic — for him, the team and me! I never spoke to Phil about it afterward. I wonder if he remembers....

After the 1995 Vuelta, my schedule took me to the world championships, in Colombia. It wasn't a trip I was looking forward to. The uncertainty of having to work in a distant country, where the European teams couldn't take their trucks or team vehicles, left most European mechanics fearing the worst. I almost went to Colombia once before, with the Coors Light team. But just before leaving for the trip, the U.S. Government suddenly warned American tourists not to go there because of civil unrest. In 1995, I again avoided making the trip when Lance decided at the last minute that his form wasn't good enough to do the race. For me, it turned out to be a wise decision, as more than 100 bikes went missing at the Bogotá airport, leaving many teams scrambling for replacements. That was a close one!

Still, the world championships are generally one of the year's great events — particularly the 1993 world's in Oslo, Norway, which provided one of the most memorable moments of my career. I went to Oslo a few days before the race with one of the soigneurs and Lance, so he could get used to the course and prepare for the race. Lance had been going very well at the time, and we all knew he had a chance to do really well.

The day before the pro road race, we were working on the U.S. team's bikes, and all the bikes of Motorola's non-American riders — about 15 bikes in all. While tinkering with Lance's bike, we came upon a problem with the water-bottle cages. The bosses — the pieces holding the cages to the frame — were stripping out. This had happened before, and replacing the piece was a huge problem. The entire bike had to be taken apart before you could drill the piece out. And then you had to remove the bottom bracket or headset, to recover the small drilled-out pieces from within the frame.

When I saw the lower boss on Lance's bike was completely stripped out, I realized the amount of work that was ahead. I had just spent one-and-a-half hours working on his bike, and this would be the very last step. The other mechanics were waiting for me to finish what was the last bike for the day ... and the most important. I asked George to pass me the tools I needed, but when he started to looked for them he realized that he had left them at our Belgian headquarters.

After a few seconds of panic, we realized there was nothing we could do. Finally, I drilled the boss out and decided to use a screw from somewhere else ... but we couldn't find one that fit. Geoff Brown, another mechanic, eventually searched the hotel basement and found a screw on the binding of an old and forgotten wooden ski. We tapped it in and hoped for the best. The next day, Lance rode that bike to win the world title. It was a super-light $5000 titanium bicycle, with all the latest top-of-the-line equipment, including titanium cogs and bolts ... and an ancient, heavy steel bolt from a set of skis that were more than

60 years old!

It was a thrill to see Lance become world champion ... but I almost didn't make it to the finish. The road conditions that day were the slipperiest I had ever encountered. Following one of many crashes, I leapt out of the U.S. team car to change a rider's wheel ... and the Belgian team car skidded into me. I hadn't seen it coming, but I did hear the sliding noise of the car before it struck me. The driver apparently tried to make it by me, but realized he couldn't when the car started sliding. The impact forced me onto one knee and under the bumper. Scared stiff, I punched the car's hood and started screaming at the driver, not knowing that the man behind the wheel was cycling legend Eddy Merckx — who was also our Motorola bike sponsor! I probably shouldn't have screamed at him, but then he did run me over, so I didn't feel too guilty....

That title race in Oslo was my third world championship assignment. The first was in 1991, at Stuttgart, Germany, on my first-ever trip to Europe. That year, the U.S. professional team included several Coors Light riders and was managed by the American team's directeur sportif, Len Pettyjohn. We traveled to Europe 10 days before the world's, to give the riders time to acclimate to European conditions by doing a couple of races in France. After arriving in Paris, we flew down to Limoges for the start of the Tour du Limousin. Some members of the race organization met the team at the airport, where we discovered that our bikes had missed the connection from Paris. Promises were made that the bikes would be delivered to the hotel that night, but by 10 p.m. they had still not arrived — and my nerves were starting to get the better of me.

The hotel owner kept assuring me that the bikes would arrive. I waited ... and waited ... while jet lag and stress took control, before I fell into a deep sleep. Then, at 3 a.m., I was woken up by the phone ringing. A quick burst of self-orientation and a double espresso later, I found that all the bikes had arrived. With no time to waste, I immediately began working on them for the race, due to start in a few hours. Most of the bikes were in pretty bad shape from the long trip

... but I had them all ready by 6:30 a.m.

When the soigneurs and Len got up, we worked out our plans for the days ahead. The race organization had given us a small passenger minivan and a car that looked ready for the junk heap, rather than a bike race. At least 10 years old, the car was not really roadworthy and, furthermore, had a rusty, homemade bike rack on top that carried three bikes upside down, and fastened with a bungie cord. How we didn't lose a bike baffles me, as did the equation of fitting seven riders, a directeur sportif, a mechanic and two soigneurs into the two cars. Miraculously, the race went reasonably well for us. We stayed in terrible hotels and ate terrible food, but the race brought us some success, with Mike Engleman finishing third overall.

After the Tour du Limousin, we hauled ourselves north to Brittany, for the Grand Prix de Plouay. A Belgian team helped us get there by taking our bikes and equipment in their truck, while we rented three cars. Still, the trip was a comedy of errors not helped by the fact most of us had never been to Europe. Unfortunately, we listened to a couple of riders on the team who had spent some time in France. Their advice made things even worse, because one said that the *autoroute* tolls were super expensive, and suggested we stick to the back roads. Of course, we took his advice and, of course, it all went wrong. A six-hour drive turned into 10! On top of that, we ignored rule No. 1 of sticking together when traveling and went our different ways.

Driving in a foreign land with three bike riders in the back was quite an ordeal. My only "help" was a road map, our hotel address in Brittany, and a few francs in my pocket. Partway through the long drive, I was distracted by a man standing in the middle of the highway waving. Approaching him, I saw it was a gendarme waving us to pull over. I stopped behind his motorcycle on the shoulder and waited for him to walk up to us. Not understanding what he said, I responded: "Je ne parle pas français" — my standard line. In reply, he simply stuck a piece of paper in my face with "650 francs" written on it. All I had

was 425 francs. After a few more minutes of trying to converse, Alexi
Grewal, who spoke some French, stepped in to explain that we were in
a pro cycling team from the U.S. and that we were here for a race.

I don't think he believed us, until Alexi explained that he was the 1994
Olympic champion, and showed him his identification. The name
seemed to ring a bell with the gendarme, especially as Alexi had raced in
Europe before with the Dutch Panasonic and French RMO teams. This
prompted the gendarme to radio a colleague, who soon arrived and discussed how I didn't have enough money to pay for the ticket. We
thought we were on the verge of a breakthrough when the second gendarme approached us (that is, until he explained in broken English that
if we didn't come up with the money they would impound the car). Just
as suddenly, Alexi pulled out some cash that he had been sitting on the
entire time, and gave them the rest of the money. I just about killed him!
I guess he was holding out to see if we could get away with it.

A couple of hours later, I found the hotel and settled in; only to discover the next day that we had to change hotels — an ordeal that took
Len Pettyjohn and I five trips to transfer all the equipment. While
working on the bikes, I noticed a small line on the inside of the right
chainstay of Mike Engleman's bike. Further inspection revealed that it
was a crack working its way around the tube. The bike would never
make it through the next day's race, let alone the world's.

Fortunately, I had brought one spare bike and it was Michael's —
although his spare bike was a pretty old and heavy one he had used for
training during the spring. The bike that had broken was a nice light
one … but obviously a little too light for European racing. It took two
hours to overhaul his spare and get it in good enough shape to race on
the next day. A replacement bike for the world's took a little longer.…
I called Coors Light's U.S. bike sponsor, Ben Serotta, who said he
could have another one ready and to me in time for the world's.

The next morning, there was bumper-to-bumper traffic on the way
to the Plouay race. Our French driver explained that it was due to peo-

ple heading to the event. When we finally got to the start, I was completely blown away by the size of the crowds. I had never seen anything like this before. Before the start of that race, I remember looking at the crowds and seeing four helicopters hovering above, and thinking, "This is pro bike racing!"

The race was super-hard and most of our guys got shelled. That night, as I was packing up for our departure the next morning, Len came into the room and said that Davis Phinney had mentioned that our flight to Paris the next day — en route to Stuttgart — might be a small plane. He was concerned the bikes again might not make it. To the dismay of the soigneurs, we had to rent a cargo van and drive it with all the bikes and our equipment to Paris instead of flying. We made it to Paris without a problem, and the flight to Stuttgart went without a hitch. And our hotel there was a decent one, too. Finally, things were working out!

Greg LeMond, Andy Hampsten and Mike Carter were the last team members for the U.S. team to arrive. Greg had his personal mechanic and soigneur with him, which I appreciated. His mechanic, a Belgian named Julian De Vries, was once Eddy Merckx's personal mechanic. A wealth of knowledge, De Vries spent a lot of time talking with me while we worked on the bikes, and he ended up working for Motorola in 1995.

The day before the world's, Len came to my room and said he had something to tell me that I wouldn't be too happy about. The U.S. team manager said he didn't want me following the pro road race in the team car, because I didn't have enough experience. He wanted De Vries in the car. I was devastated. I had busted my butt to earn the right to be at the world championships, not only over the last week but for the previous two years; and now I wasn't even going to get to ride in the team car. I was livid.

After Len left, Julian, who overheard the entire conversation, told me not to worry and that he would make sure I got to do some of the race. That he would do that for me really impressed me, and I always respected him for it. Eventually, I rode in the team car for most of the race.

Unfortunately, we had only two finishers — Hampsten and Engleman. As for Greg, he crashed out, but he wasn't in good form anyway.

In hindsight, I can understand the manager's fears about my lack of experience. If Greg had been going better that year, and had a good chance to win, it would have been the right decision to have Julian do the race. He would have been much better equipped to handle any problems that Greg may have had, especially as Julian was familiar with him and his bikes.

It was after meeting George Noyes in Europe later that year, that I agreed to work with Motorola in Europe in 1992. So, although my first trip to Europe had been very hard and in some ways miserable, it is one that I will always remember for having steered me toward my dream of working for one of the world's top pro teams.

After the world championships, the season starts its final run home. There would be the midweek Paris-Bourges race, then Paris-Tours, the second-to-last World Cup race of the year. That is a pretty flat yet very long race, usually won by the sprinters. Then it was down to Italy for the final trip of the year to race Milan-Turin and the Tour of Piedmont, before the final World Cup event, the Tour of Lombardy, in mid-to-late October.

I once asked Dag-Otto Lauritzen what he considered the hardest race in the world, and he said it was the Tour of Lombardy. Liège-Bastogne-Liège probably has the most difficult course, but Lombardy can be argued as being harder, because it is contested late in the year when most riders are losing form or are burnt-out mentally and physically. Dag-Otto said it was the only World Cup race that he had never finished.

In 1995, the season was stretched — as it often seems to be — with the inclusion of the first Tour of China. For me, it was a mission from hell that I was dreading. Fortunately, someone above shared my opinion and the axe fell swiftly on any plans for the team to go. My last trip was homeward bound … and for good. I would not return to Europe for Motorola's final season in 1996.

chapter ten

Looking Back

Living, working and traveling in Europe with the Motorola team for four years was the greatest experience of my lifetime. It is an opportunity for which I will always be grateful. Many people ask me if I miss it. In some ways I do, and in others I don't. I definitely miss living in Europe and experiencing all the richness of various cultures and countries; I miss working with some of the riders, and I miss the friends I made. But I definitely don't miss the job itself. Being a team mechanic can get very mundane and routine — washing cars and bikes, fixing bikes, riding in the back of the race car, and building wheels and bikes. Even though it is carried out in different places, the work itself is almost always the same.

Of course, the job did take me to interesting places that I had never seen before. And I know that many people wonder: How can the Tour de France and Paris-Roubaix be mundane and routine? Races like those aren't, but they are just two of the few races that I really look forward to. For every Paris-Roubaix, there were 50 rinky-dink races in obscure little towns that no one wanted to be at — including the riders. One of the more frustrating aspects of a mechanic's life was when the riders weren't motivated to race — and made it clear that they didn't want to be there. As a mechanic, you still had to put in 100-percent effort, even if the riders were just going through the motions. So, after almost seven years as a pro mechanic, I felt that there was nothing left for me to achieve. I had worked on the U.S. circuit; done all the World Cup races at least a couple of times; traveled on four Tours de France, the Tour of Italy and the Tour of Spain; and been to numerous world championships.

After meeting George Noyes, the head mechanic for Motorola, at the 1991 World Championships in Stuttgart, Germany — and several phone calls a few weeks later — my wishes were confirmed. I was signed up by Motorola to work in Europe. I still remember that moment. I hung up the phone in the highway rest stop where I had stopped to call George, got back in the car and, as soon as I was on the highway, started hooping and hollering while driving at about 90 mph with all the windows open. Until that moment, I had never realized how badly I had wanted this position. I was ecstatic. My dream of going to Europe had finally come true.

I arrived in Europe thinking I already knew everything there was to know about being a mechanic, yet I learned very quickly just how wrong I was. In some ways, though, having an attitude and a streak of cockiness helped, because it made overcoming the initial culture shock during the first couple of months a lot easier. And there were many ups and downs in my first year. I had to fit in with my new surroundings, and at the same time act as professionally as I could. The variety of personalities and characters that make up a team always kept things interesting, especially when we spent so much time together. It is a very different situation from that of a normal job. When you are on the road with a pro cycling team, you are not only working with your co-workers, but you are socializing, eating and even rooming with them for weeks on end. Imagine doing that with your current co-workers, and then you'll have an idea of what I mean. Not that it was something that

I was very good at. Tempers and emotions can start to run very high after being on the road for a long time, and it's important to try and not let things get you down. You can't have people running around, freaking out on each other all the time. So for any member of a cycling team, it's vital to be easy-going.

After two years in Europe, I started to feel bored again. I had worked on nearly every major race and didn't seem to be learning a whole lot anymore. So I decided to focus my energy on other areas of the mechanics' program, trying to make our system more efficient and higher in quality, and working less on day-to-day bike stuff. I designed a tool that was revolutionary to our program that very accurately measured the rider's position on the bike. Up until then, we had used a fairly inaccurate system — that also took three times as long to carry out.

However, by the end of the third year, I had once again exhausted every source of job satisfaction and begun searching for a new challenge. I always said that the day I felt that I was only doing this for the salary would be the time to get out. If I were not having fun any more, not only would it be bad for me, but for the team as well. It is very important to have a positive attitude and enjoy what you do. A pro team mechanic's life is hard enough. There's no place for someone with a bad attitude who doesn't want to be there.

Nevertheless, I decided to work one more year, realizing that it would be my last; and I went into it focusing on the good things and enjoying each moment and place as much as possible. I also decided not to get caught up in the petty bickering and political infighting that can go on. This worked for the most part, and I enjoyed that final year. And while it was probably apparent from time to time that my heart wasn't in it, I think that in the end I accomplished my goal.

While in Europe, I had a great number of memorable experiences. The places I saw, the people I met, the experiences that I had are all unforgettable memories, certainly very different from those experienced by a regular tourist. For one thing, when you are traveling with a sports team — particularly a cycling team — in Europe, the locals are much more accepting of you, and generally more open and friendly, than they would be of a regular tourist. And most tourists never see the incredible off-the-beaten-path places we visited. Some of the small towns and villages in which we stayed in the middle of nowhere are incredible. Also, there are many things in Europe that you just can't experience elsewhere, like a good glass of red wine and slice of mellow cheese on a warm summer night in France, or an after-dinner walk through a historic section of some centuries-old city.

Many Europeans believe that Americans have no culture; the first time I heard this I was quite offended. "They don't know what they are talking about," I thought, "those arrogant French." But after a few years, I understood their outlook and in some ways began to agree with them. When I first arrived in Europe, I couldn't believe the unusual hours kept by various businesses, and how many days a week they were closed. It seemed impossible to get anything done. My bank was open from 10 a.m. to 12 p.m. and 2 p.m. to 4:30 p.m. most days. How the heck did people get their banking done? Then, stores were closed at lunchtime for at least an hour, sometimes two; and they were closed on Sundays and maybe one other day of the week, as well. It was very frustrating, to say the least.

On the second day of my first year in Belgium, the Motorola team operations manager, Noël Dejonckheere, invited me over to his house for lunch. When we pulled up to what looked like a sewing shop on a main shopping street, I was a little perplexed. After walking in and through the back of the store, I realized there was a house attached to the back where his wife's parents lived. There were six of us for lunch: Noël, his wife and daughter, his wife's parents and me. We had a huge lunch: soup, meat and potatoes, vegetables, coffee and dessert. It was an incredible meal, and I wondered whether they had done this all for me, until I asked Noël how often they did it. He replied, "Everyday, of course," except that his brother usually came, too. To think that I thought this was a long-awaited family reunion! When I lived at home, we were lucky to sit down and eat a meal together once a week. This small example made the differences in our cultures abundantly clear to me, and from that point on I appreciated Europeans a lot more.

Europeans take more time for the important things in life, like sitting down and having a meal with their family and friends. American society seems to have jumped the tracks somewhere and lost perspective on what's important in life. It's very easy to do, because everybody does it. It's much easier to hit the McDonald's drive-through than to take time to arrange, cook and attend a family meal together. There is nothing wrong with hard work, but at what price?

In my many years as a mechanic, there were many highs and lows. Following in the team car on that miserable rainy day in Oslo when Lance Armstrong came through like a star to win the 1993 World Professional Road Race Championship was incredible, as were the days when Motorola riders won stages in the Tour de France or even had the Tour's yellow leader's jersey. The first race I ever worked alone and where a Motorola man won provided a great feeling of accomplishment. Then again, one of my biggest disappointments was when Frankie Andreu almost took the final stage of the 1994 Tour de France on the Champs-Elysées in Paris. I would have given anything to have seen him win that day, rather than be caught and passed 100 meters from the finish by Frenchman Eddy Seigneur of GAN.

By far the most devastating event that ever took place in my seven years as a mechanic was, of course, the death of our Italian colleague Fabio Casartelli, after he crashed on a descent during the 1995 Tour de France. I didn't know him well. His English wasn't good and my Italian was worse, so communication was difficult, and he had been with the team for only half a year. But he was liked by everyone on the Motorola team, and he gained all of our friendship and respect in the short time he was with us. Fabio seemed eager to learn English and was unembarrassed by the mistakes he made while trying. Above all, he was quick to smile and laugh, and seemed to have that effect on others. Fabio was notorious for his bursts of loud laughter at the dinner table that would rock the entire room. I liked this, because I have a pretty boisterous laugh and I admired how he was never embarrassed by his raucous sense of humor. Fabio never held back, no matter how quiet a restaurant we were in.

He was also an excellent rider and the winner of an Olympic gold medal at Barcelona in 1992, before he turned pro. One time, after we handed a few water bottles to Fabio from the team car, the Banesto team car pulled alongside ours and the Spanish team's directeur sportif, José Miguel Echavarri, remarked how good Fabio looked on his bike. It was very true; he looked remarkable on a bike, had a great position and always looked comfortable. He rode as if he were in harmony with his bicycle, more so than almost anyone I ever saw.

Once, someone mentioned to me that Fabio was too nice a guy to be a professional bike racer. It seemed to be a strange statement at the time, but it was also very true. He was that nice a guy; there was nothing about him that you could find not to like. His sudden death was devastating for everyone and for many months the image of him lying on the ground after the crash haunted my thoughts every day.

Trying to find the answer to the question, "Why did he crash?" plagued my thoughts for weeks. On the steep downhill turn where he fell, the very steep drop-off to the right was lined with large concrete posts to stop cars from going over the edge. Even so, two riders involved in the crash still skidded off the road into the gully, and they were only saved by landing in the branches of the one tree that stood there. Had Fabio seen them go over and crashed intentionally to avoid following them? Or did he crash unintentionally and slide into the post that took his life? These questions bothered me for a long time, but I finally realized that I'd never know the answer. Professional cycling is very dangerous, and we are fortunate that accidents like this don't happen more often.

Many bicycle shop mechanics ask me how to get a job with a team. I hate to say it, but it's a pretty tough proposition. More than anything, such an opportunity only arises by your being in the right place at the right time, and like everything else in life, it's not what you know but who you know. Still, it's worth joining the mechanics' clinic at the Olympic Training Center at Colorado Springs, Colorado. You won't be instantly offered a job with a professional team, but the clinic will give you an opportunity to meet some important people in the business and make contacts.

Also, get involved with your local amateur cycling club. Donate some of your time and go with the team on one of its big race trips. You don't have to do the whole bike-wash-and-tune-up routine that I discussed earlier in this book, but just being there to support the riders in any possible way can mean a lot to them. You'll probably learn a thing or two yourself, and also have some fun. To every aspiring mechanic, the most important thing I can stress is to be safe, be prepared, stay calm no matter what, and, above all, have fun!

Naturally, I hope you, the reader, have enjoyed *Tales from the Toolbox*, and have garnered a better insight into the life of a professional cycling team and, of course, the mechanics who work on one. Life on the professional cycling circuit is unique. I have put my toolbox away after seven years as a mechanic, but the tales that have unfolded are everlasting.